RUGBYWORLD
Yearbook 2011

Editor
Ian Robertson

Photographs
Getty Images

G2 entertainment

This book has been produced for G2 Entertainment Ltd
by Lennard Books
a division of Lennard Associates Ltd
Windmill Cottage
Mackerye End
Harpenden
Herts AL5 5DR

© Lennard Associates Limited 2010

This edition first published in the UK in 2010
by G2 Entertainment Limited

EAN/ISBN 978-1-907803-99-4

Production Editor: Chris Marshall
Design Consultant: Paul Cooper
Printed and bound in Britain by Butler Tanner & Dennis Ltd

The publishers would like to thank Getty Images for providing most of the photographs for this book. The publishers would also like to thank Fotosport UK, Inpho Photography, Chris Thau and Wooden Spoon for additional material.

The views in this book are those of the author but they are general views only and readers are urged to consult the relevant and qualified specialist for individual advice in particular situations.

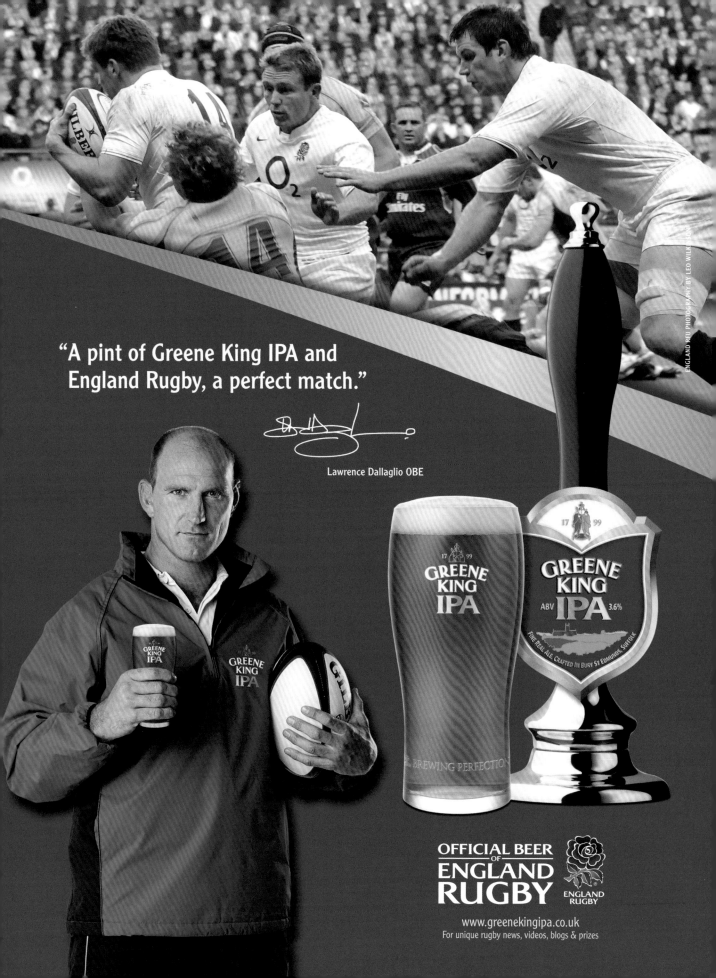

NEED A BETTER MATCH?

Let Michael Page find the right talent for your business.

We have specialised divisions in:

Actuarial	Marketing
Consultancy	Not-for-Profit
Design	Offshore
Education	Policy
Engineering & Manufacturing	Procurement & Supply Chain
Executive Interim	Property & Construction
Executive Search	Public Sector
Finance	Retail
Financial Services	Sales
Health & Social Care	Taxation
Hospitality & Leisure	Technology
Human Resources	Treasury
Legal	

We have the expertise and experience you need for top recruitment.
Contact us on 08456 007 007 to find out how we can help find the people your business needs.

As part of our ongoing commitment to Corporate Responsibility,
Michael Page International is proud to be supporting the Wooden Spoon.

Specialists in Global Recruitment
136 offices in 28 countries | www.michaelpage.co.uk

Michael Page
INTERNATIONAL

Contents

Two-thirds of the people who have ever reached 65 are alive today.

Your first great-grandchild, your second career, your third marathon.

Longer lives mean greater possibilities. The chance to explore interests, goals, the world. Time to take advantage of everything that's on offer.

Our network of 8,000 offices in 88 countries and territories means we're in a good position to help you plan for your future. And having these connections helps us realise and appreciate the richness of the world's diversity.

We're 145 years old and still going strong. Yet the possibilities we uncover for our customers are as young and fresh as ever.

HSBC

The world's local bank

FOREWORD

by HRH THE PRINCESS ROYAL

HRH The Princess Royal,
Royal Patron of Wooden Spoon.

BUCKINGHAM PALACE

Since the initial fundraising event back in 1983, Wooden Spoon has existed to add support and value to the lives of disadvantaged children and young people throughout the UK and Ireland. Over the last 27 years, hundreds of schools, hospitals, respite homes and other organisations have been able to improve their services and facilities thanks to the funds made available by Wooden Spoon.

Spoon, as it is affectionately known, has often been the quiet partner behind more visible names. This work continues unabated and the smiles of the young people whose lives have been enriched by Spoon's involvement is reward enough for all those who, through their volunteer roles, have assisted in raising funds year in year out.

In the last 18 months, even through tough economic times, Spoon has created a new and innovative programme called Spoon Community Rugby. The programme targets socially disadvantaged children and young people and uses the sport of rugby to focus their aggression and anger while developing the valuable skills of teamwork, discipline and respect. These programmes are now running throughout the country and are already delivering positive results.

However, as a charity Wooden Spoon depends heavily on corporate and individual giving to achieve its charitable objectives. At a time when the demands on charities are growing, as Patron of Wooden Spoon I invite you to lend your support to the charity that is doing so much to benefit the lives of our young people.

Anne

Wooden Spoon
The children's charity of rugby

Creating a stir for children and young people in the UK and Ireland

In the UK, one child in every hundred suffers from a lifelong disability that will profoundly affect his or her ability to lead a full and happy life.

More than 3.5 million young people grow up in low income households or live in an environment where they are subjected to poverty of aspiration.

At Wooden Spoon, we believe that all children and young people deserve the chance to live happy fulfilled lives regardless of the challenges they may face. Spoon harnesses the spirit and values of rugby to give disadvantaged children and young people in the UK and Ireland a chance to achieve their full potential in life.

Who we are:

Wooden Spoon is a children's charity founded in 1983 that is dedicated to helping underprivileged children and young people all over the UK and Ireland to live happier, richer lives.

We partner with the UK rugby community, receiving invaluable support for our activities and the opportunity to raise awareness of the work we do. In doing so, we involve some of the UK's top sporting role models in making a difference in the lives of young people in need.

We comprise over 40 regional volunteer committees as well as a central national team and we boast more than 10,000 members across the UK and Ireland. The regional committees undertake local fundraising activities and ensure that the money is spent on projects in

their community so that the benefit of our work is always immediate, visible and lasting.

During our first 25 years, over half a million young people benefitted from more than £15 million pounds of charitable support thanks to the efforts of our staff and volunteers. We are proud of our legacy, the work we do, and our ambitious plans for the future.

www.woodenspoon.com

Our vision

Wooden Spoon exists to make a positive impact on the lives of disadvantaged children and young people through our commitment to quality charitable work.

" **We take tremendous pride in the professionalism, efficiency and the 'can-do' attitude of our volunteers who make so much of our work possible.**"

Jason Leonard OBE, Lead Ambassador of Wooden Spoon

What we do

We organise our own fundraising initiatives, raise the money and spend it where it is most needed.

Over the years, our donations have diversified from purely capital projects such as medical treatment and recovery centres, sports and activity areas, sensory rooms and gardens, playgrounds and hydrotherapy pools to include outreach programmes for kids in their communities.

Some of our noteworthy projects

Wooden Spoon has funded hundreds of projects throughout the UK and Ireland. The following is a small but representative sample illustrating the scope and scale of Spoon's support for disadvantaged children and young people.

Children with cancer and leukaemia advice and support for parents (CCLASP)

Spoon donated £27,000 to pay for the refurbishment of a holiday respite cottage in Perthshire providing short-break holidays for children and their families.

Southwark Tigers

The Southwark Tigers began as a pilot project between Spoon, the RFU and Southwark Council to provide much needed activities for young people in an area of significant deprivation. By creating an opportunity for the young people of the community to play rugby, Spoon engaged young people in positive pastimes in an area that topped the national league tables for childhood obesity and teenage pregnancy.

Maesmarchog Primary School

The Special Needs Unit of this small village school in the Rhondda Valley received £20,000 from Spoon that funded the construction of a purpose-built playground for children with a range of autistic and behavioural learning difficulties.

Ace Centre

The ACE Centre in Oxford (Aiding Communication and Education) supports children with complex physical and communication disabilities. The centre was built in the grounds of the Nuffield Orthopaedic Hospital with the help of a £300,000 donation from Spoon. Here children are catered for with specific equipment and systems to help them communicate with parents, teachers and friends.

The ACE Centre is also involved in developing Stargaze, a breakthrough technology that tracks eye movements to help the severely disabled communicate and express themselves. Leicester and England U21 rugby player Matt Hampson and Spoon are proud to be involved in ongoing fundraising for the development and purchase of these systems.

The ABLE Partnership

£34,000 from Spoon paid for the construction and equipping of three greenhouses with advanced irrigation systems for growing a variety of foods. This is part of an extensive programme of education and training leading to the rehabilitation of socially and educationally excluded young people in Yorkshire.

The Cedar Foundation

Spoon donated £120,000 to this Foundation, which provides an extensive range of facilities to the disabled children of Northern Ireland, for the rebuilding and re-equipping of a building that is now the Foundation's flagship operation in the Province.

Spoon Community Rugby

Spoon Community Rugby is a series of charitable projects designed to give disadvantaged children around the UK a better chance in life by playing rugby. Rugby gives kids of all shapes and sizes a valuable role in the team, enhancing their health and self-confidence. It is particularly important for some of the most disenfranchised young people in our society who are in desperate need of guidance and physical release. By playing a sport that channels their energy into healthy activity while fostering teamwork, discipline and respect, these young people can change their lives for the better.

What events do we run?

Spoon fundraisers

Spoon's volunteer committees organise hundreds of events every year including fundraising dinners, golf events, rugby matches, balls and other assorted events that allow us to raise money and attract the attention of potential supporters. These events also offer Spoon members the chance to contribute directly and network. Much of our impressive growth of members and sponsors is directly related to our event activity.

Spoon Challenges:

A series of physical challenges that occur across the UK where people can get involved and raise money for Spoon. Events include:

Great Lakeland Challenge

The longest, highest and steepest challenge. Participants kayak England's longest lake, cycle England's steepest passes and conquer England's highest peak - all in less than 12 hours.

Four Peaks Challenge

Our most successful and well-known challenge. Participants climb four of the highest mountains in Scotland, England, Wales and Ireland, a total of 14,000 feet and drive the 1,900 miles between them - all within 48 hours.

Summer Bike Fest

Participants cycle from start points at Rugby Clubs as far afield as London and Cardiff to converge on our very own 'Henge' to watch the sun come up on the longest day.

End 2 End Cycle Challenge

One of our most taxing challenges, participants hit the roads on two wheels to cycle the length of the UK from John O'Groats to Land's End, covering more than 850 miles in only 8 days.

Wooden Spoon Lead Ambassador

Our Lead Ambassador is Jason Leonard OBE, England's most capped player and World Cup winner. Jason is not only a testament to the sporting values of rugby, but he credits his involvement with rugby at a young age with transforming his life for the better. Having gained so much from playing a sport he loves, Jason uses his voice and influence to develop Wooden Spoon's work and help the less fortunate.

Wooden Spoon Ambassadors

Wooden Spoon enjoys the support of numerous rugby legends and industry leaders who contribute their time and energy to raise awareness of Spoon's activities and help us to generate funds.

Sporting Partners

Wooden Spoon enjoys strong relationships with a variety of clubs, league associations and governing bodies to achieve our common goal of giving back to the community while using sport as a way to improve the quality of life for young people.

Our Royal Patron

Our Royal Patron is HRH The Princess Royal who gives generously of her time.

Our Rugby Patrons

The RFU, WRU, SRU, IRFU, RFL all support us in our charitable work.

Corporate Partners

Wooden Spoon has the generous support of a number of companies whose contributions enable us to change the lives of more young people in a variety of ways.

Wooden Spoon
The children's charity of rugby

41 Frimley High Street, Frimley, Surrey, GU16 7HJ

Tel: 01276 410 180 Fax: 01276 410 181 Email: charity@woodenspoon.com

www.woodenspoon.com • www.spoonchallenges.com

Charity Registration No. 326691
(England & Wales)
and SC039247 (Scotland)

Strutt&Parker&CountryHomes
&Commercial&Farming&Land
Management&BuildingSurveying
&Leisure&Hotels&Estate&Farm
Agency&Accounting&Taxation
&Planning&Development&
Valuations&BuyingService&
SportingAgency&ResidentialSales
&Lettings&proud supporters of
the Wooden Spoon.

Strutt & Parker. The nationwide property specialist that offers
a complete service through our network of over 45 offices.

www.struttandparker.com

Governing Rugby
125 Years of the IRB

by **CHRIS THAU**

'The three founding unions decided to suspend their fixtures against England at the third meeting of the board, on 5 December 1887, until such time as England agreed to join'

In 2011 the world of rugby celebrates 125 years since the formation of the International Board. In 1886, when the board was conceived, international rugby exchanges, which had started with the match between England and Scotland in 1871, were confined to the four Home Unions, with the Rugby Football Union, the holders of the laws of the game, very much the dominant force.

The process that led to the formation of the board had commenced in 1884, with a disputed try in the match between England and Scotland on 1 March, at Blackheath. According to various records, during the course of the game one of the Scottish players, Charles Berry, knocked a ball back, which was gathered by Richard Kindersley of England, who scored a try. The Scottish players argued that it was illegal to knock the ball back. The English replied that irrespective of whether it was illegal or not, and in their opinion knocking a ball back was not illegal, a team may not be allowed to take advantage of their own mistake – an early statement of the advantage law.

After long deliberations – 'for the best part of half an hour, the players stood about the field not knowing what to do' – the referee, George Scriven, a former captain of Ireland, eventually awarded the try to England despite the protestations of the Scots. Wilfred Bolton converted and England won by one goal to one try, scored for Scotland by J. Jamieson. After the match, Scotland suggested adjudication, but England rejected the proposal, arguing that the decision of the referee – the sole judge – should be allowed to stand.

However, the Scots felt so strongly about it that the fixture was cancelled the following season, despite the correspondence between the two unions. The secretary of the Irish union, H.G. Cook, proposed that representatives of the four unions should meet and discuss the outstanding issues and that consideration should be given to the formation of an International Board 'for the settlement of international disputes'. The RFU agreed and took part in a conference alongside Scotland and Ireland in Dublin on 6 February 1886. The board came into existence in 1886 sometime after the meeting. It was known as the International Rugby Football Board (IRFB) until 1998, when it became simply the International Rugby Board (IRB).

The first meeting of the board, with former Scotland full back James Carrick in the chair and his countryman J.A. Gardner as secretary, was held in Manchester in 1887. Ireland were represented by E. McAlister and Thomas Lyle, while from Wales came Richard Mullock and former international Horace Lyne, who went on to serve on the board for a record 51 years until his retirement in 1938. Following the Dublin conference, Scotland had awarded the disputed 1884 match to England, on the understanding that the RFU would join an International Board composed of an equal number of representatives of each of the four unions. That was not the case, as England felt, rightly or wrongly, that given the size of their union and the number of English clubs, their representation should be bigger. Also the RFU, who were the game's lawmakers at the time, refused to allow the International Board control of the laws of the game. Interestingly enough, the second board meeting, chaired by E. McAlister, was attended by the RFU's George Rowland Hill, though not in a 'representative capacity'.

The three founding unions decided to suspend their fixtures against England at the third meeting of the board, on 5 December 1887, until such time as England agreed to join. The decision was reinforced by a resolution on 29 September 1888 that 'no International match with England can take place until the English Rugby Union agrees to join the International Board'. As a result there were no matches between England and the three unions for two seasons, until 1890 when the four agreed to refer the matter to arbitration. In fact, even before the arbitrators were elected and made their decision known, England had rejoined the championship, on the understanding, without prejudice to the settlement of the dispute, that the international matches should be played under the rugby laws of the country in which each match took place. This was mostly due to the diligent efforts of the players themselves, who at the time were referees as well as administrators.

The arbitrators, Lord Kingsburgh, who was Scotland's Lord Justice Clerk, and Major Francis Marindin, the president of the Football Association, ruled in favour of England, who were given six seats on the board, matching the six of the other three unions combined, which meant that England could never be outvoted by the other three. Significantly, the adjudicators also ruled that 'all international matches shall be played by the laws approved by the Board'. The level

FACING PAGE England against Scotland is the oldest fixture on the international card. However, a disputed try in 1884 caused a rift between the two unions and led to the formation of the International Board.

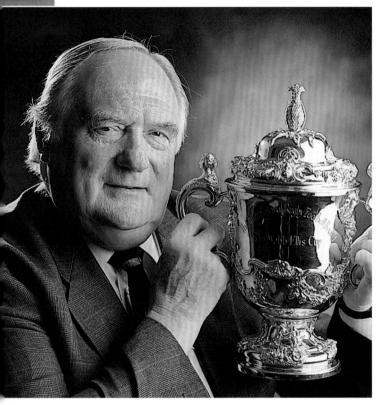

of English representation on the board remained unchanged until 1911, when the RFU, reacting to a proposal by Scotland, agreed to reduce its representation from six to four. One of the earliest and arguably most significant decisions of the 12-strong board, under the chairmanship of former England captain E. Temple Gurdon (another board stalwart who represented England as a member for 38 years), was to allocate points to the game's various forms of scoring at the February 1892 meeting.

It is worth pointing out that until after World War II, the leading overseas unions – the New South Wales Union (formed in 1874), the Queensland Rugby Union (1878), the South African Rugby Board (SARB; 1889) and the New Zealand Rugby Union (NZRU; 1892) – were members of the RFU, and as such had no representation on the IRFB, being represented by the English union. After the war, RFU representation was reduced to two to enable the admission of the NZRU, the SARB and the newly formed Australian Rugby Union (ARU) to the IRFB with an allocation of one seat each. This arrangement lasted until 1958, when it was agreed that all seven member unions would have two representatives each. France joined the board in 1978.

In 1982, a proposal to hold a World Cup tournament was discussed at the IRFB General Meeting and a year later the ARU suggested that plans for such a tournament be further investigated. Three proposals for a World Cup tournament were received by the board from three member unions in 1983, and in 1984 the board agreed that New Zealand and Australia should prepare a feasibility study for consideration in 1985. On 21 March 1985, at the IRFB General Meeting in Paris, it was 'resolved to hold a RWC [Rugby World Cup] tournament on a trial basis'. The KDD Rugby World Cup held in New Zealand and Australia in 1987 was a great success and led to the successful continuation of the tournament on a four-yearly basis.

In 1986, the centenary year of the IRFB, the board agreed to expand, and invited the rest of the playing world to join as associate members. Associate membership was a short-lived administrative option, as very soon afterwards full membership was granted to all playing nations. In 1988, after the first RWC, a permanent full-time IRFB secretariat, with former Wales international and Lions Test player Keith Rowlands as general secretary, was installed temporarily in London, then moved to Bristol; it is now in Dublin. Meanwhile, the RWC tournament became a permanent feature of the international sporting calendar.

The success of RWC 1987 paved the way for RWC 1991, held in the UK, Ireland and France. RWC 1991 gave a glimpse of the huge commercial potential of the game, but more significantly, and unlike the previous 'by invitation only' RWC tournament, it was open to all unions with IRFB membership. The meritocratic nature of the event fired the imaginations of the smaller nations, who flocked in to join the IRFB. The numbers grew steadily from 1991 when 46 unions took part in the tournament, including the qualifying rounds, to RWC 2007, in which 96 unions participated overall. Meanwhile, in 1995 the board had declared the game 'open', and in 2009 the spread and development of rugby was given a further boost with its readmission to the Olympics – Sevens will feature at the 2016 games in Rio de Janeiro.

Radix Malorum Est Cupiditas

by PAUL STEPHENS

'This season's list of fixtures for the British & Irish Cup has been published. Bristol are facing the trip to Melrose in February when there is the likelihood of snow lying round and about'

ABOVE Full back Luke Arscott crosses for Bristol against Exeter Chiefs at Sandy Park in the first leg of the 2009-10 Championship play-off final, only for the try to be disallowed.

With bricklayers, miners and plumbers meeting bankers and solicitors on equal terms in meaningful rugby union, after the declaration to accept professionalism in 1995, the sweet aroma of gold was in the air. For some, though not all, it was deliciously refreshing. Apart from the unique structure and widespread allure of amateur rugby union, there was the fascination of the game and for the fellowship. This is now mere history to be replaced by money and sponsorship. Many would say that is has not been worth it.

With the door to professionalism ajar, what we thought would be a flow of interest soon turned into an unstoppable torrent. The entrepreneurs and big spenders had arrived; many were soon being courted by those with the interests of ambitious clubs at heart. The birth pangs were in some cases excruciatingly painful. Tony Hallett, then the secretary of the Rugby Football Union, called the decision to adopt professionalism 'A burning of Rugby's vanities'.

The introduction of a paid game for the smaller clubs was a troubled time for many of them, some of whom were desperate to come to terms with the new arrangements. Division Two – or the Championship as it is grandly titled – is desperately short of funds. Many of the clubs have been obliged to expand and develop their commercial activities to stay afloat. Of those who contested the last Courage League Premiership in 1997-98, only Bath, Leicester, Saracens, Wasps and Gloucester have avoided the drop into a lower division, or insolvency. The upheaval, turmoil and disorder in English club rugby is only the beginning of the story. It goes much, much deeper.

A lot has happened in this fateful period. The club scene is minus several famous names. West Hartlepool have surrendered their ground, as have Moseley, Coventry, Birmingham/Solihull and Nottingham. Roundhay and Headingley lost theirs too, to sign up with Premiership new boys Leeds, and a lot of good it has done them, including relegation three times. Saracens, Bristol, Wasps, Sale and London Irish have taken to staging their home games in football stadia. Otherwise they may have had to join Orrell and Wakefield in liquidation. Others such as Liverpool, Richmond, Northern and London Scottish have had to seek a new status as the game has changed.

Francis Baron, who was the chief executive officer of the RFU, refused to bail out clubs, insisting that their long-term viability is not an issue for those without a sustainable business model. 'We have tried to encourage clubs at all levels that the number one rule in business is to live within your means,' said Baron.

In September 2009, while the rugby world still reverberated to the 'Bloodgate' episode at Harlequins which disfigured the club game that year, the RFU launched its 'This is Rugby' campaign based on the findings of its Core Values Task Group, which had been at work since 2007 looking into a perceived decline in behaviour in the sport. The RFU had established the task group 'to evaluate what the game stood for and what it should represent in the

LEFT Francis Baron, then chief executive officer of the Rugby Football Union, faces the media at the launch of the RFU's 'This is Rugby' Core Values campaign at Twickenham Stadium in September 2009.

FACING PAGE RFU tournaments and competitions director Terry Burwell at the Millennium Stadium in Cardiff for the May 2009 launch of the British & Irish Cup.

future', and the project identified five key ingredients 'that lie at the heart of rugby in England'. These were: Teamwork, Respect, Enjoyment, Discipline and Sportsmanship. The foundation of rugby union is sportsmanship. According to the Core Values project, 'We uphold the rugby tradition of camaraderie with teammates and opposition. We observe fair play both on and off the pitch and are generous in victory and dignified in defeat. We play to win but not at all costs and recognise both endeavour and achievement. We ensure that the wellbeing and development of individual players is central to all rugby activity.' In 1893 Arthur Budd, a former England international and erstwhile president of the RFU, wrote: 'The history of all sports over which professionalism has gained sway is a catalogue of corruptibility and decay.'

'With a brilliant stadium at Twickenham all built with our own money, we have a lot to be proud of' was Baron's take on the Quins debacle. 'But we don't want another episode like this thank you very much. Massive lessons have been learned by everyone. Not one drop of fake blood will be seen on a rugby field again.' It sounded like a good way to ease the flood of bad vibes engendered by Harlequins, not to mention the drugs issue at Bath. If only we could believe it. Some hopes.

Which brings me to what happens next. After five seasons of supporting the Premiership, Guinness have gone. Their replacement is Aviva, one of Britain's leading insurance companies, who have settled on a four-year, £20-million deal, which signifies a long-term commitment to sport and Aviva's work in the community. What should concern us all is not the Premiership but those clubs below it in the Championship and elsewhere.

When the RFU's director of elite rugby, Rob Andrew, declared at the start of last season that he would be interested in the Championship and would do all he could to help those clubs making up the second tier in the game, I doubt if he knew what he was talking about. How could he have known that Moseley, Nottingham, Coventry, London Welsh and Birmingham/Solihull would be in so much trouble? Only Exeter and Bristol were able to prove they were capable of playing in front of the big crowds which regularly attend their matches and attract 4000-plus gates. At Bedford average attendances rarely number more that 3000, while gates at Plymouth Albion, Rotherham – who have not been without their difficulties – and Cornish Pirates sometimes top 2000. Below that there is almost nothing to get excited about. With the RFU cutting its budget by £5 million, there is very little hope of more money being available from that source, so what should we do?

The Rugby Union's nugatory idea was to appoint Terry Burwell as the tournament director and instigate the British & Irish Cup. This competition, first played last season and won by Cornish Pirates who defeated a Munster second team 23-14, would be laughable were it not taken so

next

We are proud to support **The Wooden Spoon Rugby World**

www.next.co.uk

seriously by the RFU. This season's list of fixtures has been published, pitting Plymouth Albion against Leinster in Dublin during December. Bristol are facing the long trip to Melrose in February when there is the likelihood of snow lying round and about. The British & Irish Cup has no sponsor, gets no television coverage, the travel costs are extraordinary and there are no away-team followers. It is heroically tedious, valiantly uninteresting, and is meaningless in every way. It should be scrapped forthwith.

It would be much better to make the top two divisions, each of 14 clubs, as the only professional group in the game. The RFU should see that they all get infinitely more money than they do now. Below the top 28 clubs there would be no funding, with the provision that promotion and relegation remain in place, with one up and one down. Unless you have forgotten, only one club from England – Northampton – made the knockout stages of the Heineken Cup last season, leaving the French and Irish teams to dominate that competition as they have in recent years.

Below the rarefied professional elite of 28, divide the clubs into four divisions – London, North, South West and Midlands – and bring back the local derby games. This will generate greater interest and bigger gates, reduce travel expenditure, remove the need to take Saturdays off, and bring a better bar take with old friendships renewed. It should also diminish the number of clubs seeking administration. Is there any point at all in Redruth playing league rugby against Blaydon? None whatsoever.

To assist England's cause – remember they have not won a Grand Slam once since 2003 – should we perhaps go the whole hog and return to the Divisional Championship with only the England-qualified players being eligible to play in it?

Firstly though let us remember the words of Timothy: *Radix Malorum Est Cupiditas*. Greed is the root of all evil.

BELOW Leinster A take on Cornish Pirates at Dublin's Donnybrook Stadium in round two of the 2009-10 British & Irish Cup. A crowd of 1670 watched the Pool A match, which started at 4pm on a Friday afternoon and ended in a 12-10 win for the Irish side.

A New England?
the Next Generation Steps Up

by **MICK CLEARY**

'As England's footballers showed in South Africa, you have to be primed and ready. The consequences are dismal if you are not. England have to seize the moment and back the young players'

They talked a good game. Spoke about how fab everything was behind the scenes. Told us that they were training well. Gelling. Communicating. Playing with adventure. Having no fears. All that sort of stuff. Yet much as you wanted to believe, much as you wanted to have faith in the Martin Johnson mission statement, you just couldn't deny the evidence of your own eyes. England were laboured and fractured. England were one-paced and uptight. England were reliant on their scrum. England seemed not to be on each other's radar.

And then came Sydney. Will the 21-20 victory at the Olympic Stadium be a turning point? It would be hard not to think so. It was not just that England beat the Wallabies for only the third time ever on Australian soil, the previous occasions both coming in 2003, but that they did so by playing with spirit and devil and attitude. And with several young blokes.

Are the two factors linked? Of course they are. The presence of the likes of 20-year-old Leicester scrum half Ben Youngs and 21-year-old Northampton lock Courtney Lawes was instrumental to England's more brazen approach. Slowly, England are finding a new identity. Gradually they are emerging from their shell, throwing off the inherent caution that has dogged their game.

LEFT England's Courtney Lawes tussles with Rocky Elsom of the Wallabies during the summer's Second Test at Sydney, which England won 21-20.

FACING PAGE Lawes's fellow Saint Chris Ashton runs away to score England's second try at Sydney.

Martin Johnson has begun to realise that. His coaches have begun to realise that. And the reason is simple. England have absolutely no chance of victory at the 2011 Rugby World Cup in New Zealand if they go there intent only on playing the percentages. The game has moved on this year, and rapidly so. It took time for Johnson's management to log in to that. But the penny has dropped. There has to be pace and cleverness, there has to be a willingness to counterattack, there has to be slack in the system, so that if players fancy having a crack, they can do just that.

That's exactly what Youngs did when he saw an Aussie forward drift off the back of a line out, leaving an inviting hole through which the England scrum half scampered with great glee all the way to the try line. Chris Ashton's try only ten minutes later was born of the same instinct. The Northampton wing saw the possibilities and set off at a rate of knots once lock Tom Palmer had delivered the deftest of inside passes.

Of course, England had to rely on several other factors in that Test match in Sydney. Their scrum was once again dominant if not quite as overpowering as it had been in Perth the previous week. There was also the little matter of Wallaby centre Matt Giteau missing a sitter from in front of the sticks with just ten minutes to go. (Mind you, Jonny Wilkinson also fluffed what for him was a routine pot at the posts two minutes from time.) England rode their luck. And there's nothing wrong with that. But you've got to be in a position whereby you might get the rub of the green.

England have to take this attitude with them into the autumn and beyond. If they don't, then we're back to the dog days when we're not sure what sort of England might turn up. We've been here before, notably in the aftermath of the 2010 Six Nations Championship. Remember? England had run Grand Slam France close in Paris, only losing 12-10. There was real energy in their performance that night, a sense that they were throwing caution to the wind and taking advantage of a nervous display from France as they looked to close in on an historic moment themselves.

And then what? Fast-forward to the First Test at the Subiaco Oval in Perth and England were a throwback to the bad old days, when bash-and-grunt rugby was their default mode. They only managed to hang on in during that match because of a ridiculous disparity in the respective scrums. Australia were beyond woeful. They might now have two decent international props in Ben Alexander and Benn Robinson, both of whom were missing through injury, but their back-ups are inadequate. Quite rightly, England played to that strength. But even they recognised that if victory had accrued from that phase – and two penalty tries had never been seen before in a Test between

the major powers – then it would have been in many ways an empty victory. It would have brought England nothing but a win in a Test match. It would have served no useful purpose for the future, for those circumstances would never arise again. If anything, it might have led England down a cul-de-sac of misguided belief in their own prowess.

So, how is it that a measly one-point victory might be heralded as something significant? Easy. Because of the manner in which it was achieved and because of the personnel who helped bring it about. The England coaches now have empirical evidence at their fingertips. They now have proof that backing the youngsters is not a reckless gamble but the only way to go. New Zealand groomed several newcomers during the early stages of their season, players such as Israel Dagg, Aaron Cruden and Benson Stanley. England have to follow suit. If there's one sure thing that they have learned from the summer tour, it is that the next generation has to be blooded. For Ben Youngs and Courtney Lawes in Australia, read the likes of Saracens duo full-back-cum-fly-half Alex Goode and open-side Andy Saull. There are others gathering at the edges. Gloucester lock Dave Attwood was impressive for the midweek side in Australia. He needs exposure at Test level. Prop Paul Doran-Jones, Attwood's team-mate at Kingsholm, also showed that his call-up to the senior side last November was not just a selection hand forced by extreme levels of injury.

England have always had players at their disposal. What they have never been particularly good at is bringing those players through at the right time. The November series of Test matches is a perfect opportunity for England to integrate these players into the main squad as they prepare for the games against Samoa and the big three southern hemisphere powers, New Zealand, South Africa and Australia. There are no more tours now before the Rugby World Cup itself in September 2011. England will play a few warm-up matches in July and August, but these games are designed to fine-tune not to sift talent. That process has to be well under way by then.

England are in a decent place. Scotland did terrifically well on their trip to Argentina, but it is England's result in Sydney that really stands out. The coaches now have to build on that platform. They have to seize the initiative and make the benefit of that victory count for something as the World Cup approaches. As England's footballers showed in South Africa, you have to be primed and ready. The consequences are dismal if you are not. England have to seize the moment and back the young players.

BELOW Alex Goode crosses for England Saxons in the 2010 Churchill Cup final in Harrison, New Jersey. The Saracen can play at No. 10 or No. 15.

FACING PAGE Having stepped up to the captaincy against France in the 2010 Six Nations, Lewis Moody shone in the role in Australia and is set to skipper England in the autumn.

ÔNORTON ROSE

Sponsors of Southern Hemisphere rugby on Sky Sports

INTERNATIONAL
SCENE

Handling the Pressure
the All Blacks and RWC 2011

by RAECHELLE INMAN

'Unlike any other nation, the success or otherwise of its rugby team is integral to the national psyche. New Zealand is a small country and the All Blacks give it world status'

When asked how they are feeling about Rugby World Cup 2011, Richie McCaw and Graham Henry both responded without hesitation with the same word: 'Excited!' The explanation of the All Black coach is interesting, 'I have been involved in two World Cups before, one with New Zealand and one with Wales, and whether you like it or not it is the pinnacle of what we are trying to achieve. We [the All Blacks] have a reasonably high success rate outside of that but we haven't had a high success rate in Rugby World Cups. It's a real challenge for the All Blacks and those involved in the All Blacks and so that makes it exceptionally exciting as the expectations are huge.'

The Kiwis have been accused many times of 'choking' in World Cups, so why, in Henry's opinion, has the New Zealand powerhouse only been victorious in one World Cup, the inaugural tournament all the way back in 1987?

'Each time there have been different circumstances. I think sides try to peak for Rugby World Cups and perhaps the All Blacks take every game they play exceptionally seriously and try to win all of those games and so maybe our focus hasn't been entirely on Rugby World Cup … so I guess it's trying to make sure we get the balance right this time,' he commented.

'Rugby in New Zealand has always had huge expectations. Every game we are expected to win, and expected to win well, and that's not realistic. But I think it's also good for us as I think it brings the best out of the people involved, the players, the management and so on, so I think that expectation is a positive and we have to embrace it and get on with it,' Henry revealed.

Looking at the situation like this is definitely the best way to cope with the unparalleled amount of pressure. Unlike any other nation, the success or otherwise of its rugby team is integral to the national psyche. New Zealand is a small country and the All Blacks give it world status; their performance is a sign of success of the entire nation. The media and the public in New Zealand are unforgiving when the team doesn't win. Absolutely everyone in New Zealand has an opinion on the All Blacks. 'I think you've got to make sure that your development steps are right and you're progressing as a team and that you don't take anything for granted. You have to make sure that you prepare for every game as best you can and never go into a game with any false impressions or illusions,' Henry continued.

When asked if he felt complacency had been a problem with the All Blacks in the past, Henry responded emphatically: 'No. I think that's a figment of people's imaginations. I know that's been stated before, but I have only been involved in one All Black World Cup campaign before and we certainly weren't complacent playing France in Cardiff in 2007. It was just one of those games where things didn't bounce our way.'

ABOVE Coach Graham Henry chats with rising star Israel Dagg after the latter was picked to make his All Black debut against Ireland in June 2010.

FACING PAGE Cory Jane and Mils Muliaina celebrate a score in the All Blacks' 31-17 pounding of the Springboks in Wellington in July, which followed a 32-12 win over the world champions the previous week. Can the All Blacks replicate such form at the World Cup?

LEFT Skipper McCaw rallies his troops during the June 2010 Test against Wales at the Waikato Stadium, which the All Blacks won 29-10.

Having played in two World Cups, McCaw is obviously scarred by the team's inability to bring home the Webb Ellis Cup; the shock quarter-final exit in 2007 in particular remains fresh in his memory. The desperation and the burden of expectation are evident in the skipper's voice. 'There's definitely pressure involved and you could argue that it had an impact especially at the last one [World Cup] … all teams there are under pressure to perform, especially the teams that are expected to perform well, so it's whoever deals with it best and maybe we didn't last time,' McCaw admitted.

In contrast there were absolutely no expectations of the Kiwi soccer side, the All Whites, in the 2010 FIFA World Cup in South Africa, where they performed remarkably well. Although they didn't proceed past the pool stage, they were unbeaten in the tournament, recording respectable draws with the experienced, professional teams of Italy, Slovakia and Paraguay. This success was exciting for the country but simply a blip, and was soon replaced again by the All Blacks in New Zealand's sporting consciousness.

'I don't think it has taken too much focus off rugby, I think Kiwis watched with a hell of a lot of interest and from my point of view it's awesome to see them [the All Whites] do what they did. They did way better than anyone expected and that was pretty cool … sometimes the media ask if we're worried no one will support the All Blacks any more but you can support both,' McCaw commented.

He feels that his side can learn from the All Whites in their own quest for World Cup glory. McCaw believes having many players in the current All Black squad who have played in one or two World Cups is a competitive advantage. 'We have been through some pretty tough times in the last couple [of World Cups] with disappointments, so I would have hoped we've learnt from them. As the national sport you have to deal with pressure and there's no better place for having to learn to deal with it than at the World Cup … so hopefully those experiences will mean that we will be able to handle things better this time.

'I think that being able to consistently go out and perform in each situation is the art of top-level sport. You look at all sports at this level and the teams that can handle those situations and perform no matter what is going on around them, they're the ones that succeed and we work on trying to achieve that consistency.'

The All Black captain's excitement is driven by the fact that his country will fully host their very first World Cup. The 1987 Rugby World Cup final was played at Auckland's Eden Park, although the Kiwis co-hosted the tournament overall with Australia. And the 2003 World Cup was originally planned to be shared again by the two nations, but all games were shifted to Australia following a contractual dispute over ground signage rights between the New Zealand Rugby Football Union and Rugby World Cup Limited and this contentious disappointment still seems fairly raw for the Kiwis.

'I am excited about the World Cup as it comes around pretty quick and there's a bit of hype in New Zealand, people are starting to talk about it more and that makes it quite exciting.

'The usual talk from some people is around pressure but I think it will be great; it's familiar to us and friends and family are around, so it will mean we can just get on and worry about the rugby and enjoy it. Not having to travel will be a bit of an advantage.'

Henry agrees: 'I think home advantage is a factor and that should help the All Blacks ... and from a big-picture point of view it is great for the country and I think the people of New Zealand are getting excited about that and, although New Zealand rugby will lose money out of it, which is ridiculous, the New Zealand economy will obviously benefit and it will put New Zealand on the map again, which is important.'

The country is investing in upgrades and infrastructure, with improvements such as Eden Park's new six-level, 21,500-seat South Stand at a cost of NZ$256 million. The stadium will have a permanent capacity of 50,000, with an additional 10,000 temporary seats for the World Cup.

Henry's focus right now is on the All Blacks' Test against the Wallabies in Hong Kong and the subsequent tour to the United Kingdom at the end of 2010. 'After the end-of-year tour this year we don't see the players for about seven or eight months as they are playing in a different competition for regional sides throughout New Zealand and so that is extremely difficult. We are trying to work with the franchise coaches so we're all on the same page,' Henry explained.

'We visit the franchises quite often, so we are talking to the individual players on a pretty regular basis ... the northern hemisphere sides are obviously playing in the Six Nations [during the Super 15 tournament] and we keep an eye on what's happening there.

'As the time frame decreases towards the World Cup we will be more focused on that – at the moment we are just trying to ensure we have some players that play well.'

McCaw sees the right mix of youth and experience and the culture of the side as vital in preparation. 'Between now and the World Cup it will be about building a team that plays for each other and when it gets really tough they put everything they can into it, and that doesn't just happen straightaway. That's been going on for the last couple of years, and each time you come together you hope to add to it.'

Critical to their World Cup success is selecting the best squad available as well as having key players fit and at their peak. 'I think a guy like Dan Carter in a role like No. 10 has to make sure he plays well and we need to make sure we help him with that. If he directs the play well he will stand out,' McCaw commented.

But such reliance on one player is dangerous. If Carter is injured it won't be good news for the All Blacks. Henry's clear choice of back-up is Aaron Cruden, but he considers Steve Donald, Nick Evans and Luke McAlister as other potential options.

The World Cup has a reputation for creating stars. Who will be discovered in 2011?

'I can't think of anyone that you haven't heard of who will take the world by storm but you never know it could be a Sonny Bill Williams,' said McCaw.

Williams was once one of rugby league's brightest young talents, before switching to rugby union in 2008 in controversial circumstances, walking out only one year into a five-year contract with Canterbury Bulldogs in Australia's National Rugby League.

After two years playing in France, Williams has signed on for the Canterbury Crusaders in New Zealand, where he will play alongside Carter in the 2011 Super 15, but still has to prove himself at the highest level of rugby. It is clear that his goal is to represent the All Blacks in the World Cup.

'Sonny Bill Williams is a hell of an athlete and some of the guys I know who have played against him in Europe have said he's come to rugby pretty well, so he's going to give himself the best shot next year and we've all got to help him. If he's up to it and performs I don't see why he can't make it – I guess time will tell,' McCaw said.

Henry is even more positive about Williams' potential: 'It's highly possible Sonny Bill Williams will be part of our World Cup plans.

'He said to me that he wouldn't have come back to New Zealand unless he thought he was going to be good enough, so he didn't want to embarrass himself and others by attempting a goal that he didn't think was achievable ... I have been highly impressed by the maturity and modesty of what he has said in the media. He hasn't blown his own

BELOW Sonny Bill Williams in action for Toulon in the 2010 Amlin Challenge Cup final, in which he was man of the match.

trumpet. He realises he has a huge challenge ahead of him and he is looking forward to giving it his best shot … It appears as though he is going to be a real contender.'

Williams turned down a reported £1.34 million from Toulon to follow his boyhood dream of playing for the All Blacks. He will have good insight into the players who will represent France, a team which has been a thorn in the New Zealand side, shattering the Kiwis' chances in the quarter-final of the last World Cup and also in the semi-finals in 1999.

In 2011 the All Blacks have been drawn in the same pool as France, a pool which also includes Tonga, Canada and Japan. 'The pool is tricky, because you are expected to have games that are fairly straightforward, but this time we have France in our pool … It will make it interesting, especially with the history between New Zealand and France at World Cups … and the Tongans are always pretty physical,' said McCaw.

The World Cup opener at Eden Park will see the All Blacks take on their Pacific Island neighbours Tonga on 9 September 2011. The New Zealand skipper continued: 'At the end of the day I think the previous experience at the World Cups has taught us that you have to get your performance dead right effectively through your knockout games. It's three knockout games and no matter who they are you have to perform to your best, that's why it's called the World Cup.'

Henry sees that the All Blacks have many threats to realising their ambition at home. 'South Africa has been strong, Australia is developing and Robbie [Deans] is doing a job of development in that group and they will get better as they go along towards the Rugby World Cup. We have played the Welsh recently and although on paper we had relatively easy wins they had a number of players who weren't here and they were a very competitive side. The French are obviously strong and Martin Johnson will be pleased with the English development … there are a number of teams who could win.'

So, does Henry have a sense of confidence at this stage that the All Blacks have what it takes to win the next World Cup?

'Yep. I think we're doing what we need to be doing right now, making the right steps and planning to make sure we're the best we can be and then you've just got to do the business in the tournament … when it comes to the World Cup we have to treat every Test match as our last one, and do our best in it.'

McCaw agreed: 'As a player if you doubt if you're good enough you're in the back blocks from the start. You have to believe that you're good enough … I'm confident we have the players to give ourselves a really good start.

'We need to think about how we're going to succeed; the style we want to play and we also need to be flexible and adapt to what happens … the rugby you play in World Cups can be different to the way you play in other international matches and we have to make sure we figure out what's best for us. If we can do that we won't have any surprises.

'The last couple [of World Cups] we've had a pretty good chance and we haven't done it, but that's what World Cups are about, only one team can win it and there will be a lot of disappointed ones. We can't change what has happened, we just have to go into this next one realising that we've got a good chance and we have the team to do it and then give it a good crack; you can't do more than that.'

McCaw hopes to emulate David Kirk's efforts and be holding the Webb Ellis Cup aloft on his home soil at Eden Park on 23 October 2011. The New Zealanders have been patient, and if the team can turn the weight of expectation of a nation into a positive force, perhaps after 24 years of waiting their time will have come again.

Forging the Link
the 2010 Junior World Rugby Trophy
by CHRIS THAU

'The Junior World Rugby Trophy (JWRT) serves as the link between the elite Junior World Championship (JWC) and the regional age-group tournaments'

When the winning New Zealand youth team performed the haka at the end of the IRB Under 19 World Championship held in Belfast in the spring of 2007, everyone present was aware that this was the end of an era, and of course the beginning of a new age in world age-group rugby. This was the last Under 19 World Championship, bringing to an end a tradition that started in 1969 in Madrid, when the first age-group (European Under 19) rugby tournament was held, under the auspices of FIRA-AER.

From 2008, the Under 19s were to merge with the Under 21s (whose world championship had debuted only in 2002 in South Africa and was last held in France in 2006) into a new, unified Under 20 age group. Two world tournaments would be held, a Championship and a Trophy, operating on a promotion/relegation basis. The Junior World Rugby Trophy (JWRT) serves as the link between the elite Junior World Championship (JWC) and the regional age-group tournaments, the biggest and most sustainable development tool in the IRB member unions.

The new Under 20 age group made its international bow at the IRB Junior World Rugby Trophy tournament in Chile in April 2008. Eight nations qualified for the tournament: hosts Chile; Uruguay,

winners of the South American section; Jamaica, winners of the North American play-offs; Asian champions Korea; Cook Islands, winners of the Pacific play-offs; the winners and runners-up of the European section, Romania and Georgia; and Namibia, the champions of Africa. In the final, Uruguay defeated Chile 20-8 in a tightly fought game to win the Trophy for the first time, and with it promotion to the IRB Junior World Championship 2009 in Japan.

The inaugural Junior World Championship was held in Wales in June 2008, when New Zealand Under 20 confirmed their pre-tournament-favourite status to defeat England 38-3 in an exciting final at Swansea's Liberty Stadium to become the first world champions at the new Under 20 age group. The second IRB JWRT took place at Nairobi in Kenya, with Romania prevailing 25-13 over a hard and eager USA in the final, while the Championship event held in Japan last year saw a repeat of the 2008 final, with New Zealand defeating a talented England side once again in an intensely fought, occasionally dramatic match that ended 44-28.

Before the 2009 JWRT tournament in Kenya was concluded, it was announced that the Championship competition was to be restructured, the number of participants being reduced from 16 to 12. That sent Romania, winners of the 2009 Trophy tournament, back to the 2010 Trophy contest in Moscow, alongside newcomers Russia, Zimbabwe and Papua New Guinea and four former Championship contenders in Canada, Japan, Italy and Uruguay.

JWRT 2010 was the first IRB tournament held in Russia, a true reflection of the progress of rugby in the country, which will feature at RWC 2011 in New Zealand, having qualified for the final tournament of the Rugby World Cup for the first time. At the captains' photocall at Ismailovo shortly

ABOVE Russia's Stanislav Selskiy (centre) cradles the IRB Junior World Rugby Trophy, flanked by the captains of the two previous winners – Uruguay's Sebastián Sagario (with beard) and Romania's Petru Tamba. Behind stand the captains of the remaining participants in Moscow (left to right): Jackson Pato Jr (Papua New Guinea), Graham Kaulback (Zimbabwe), Andrew Crow (Canada), Tommaso Benvenuti (Italy) and Kota Yamashita (Japan).

FACING PAGE Action from the seventh-place play-off between Papua New Guinea and Zimbabwe.

before the tournament kick-off, the JWRT trophy itself made a public appearance, while the matches were held at two traditional rugby venues – the Slava and Fili stadia. The eight teams arrived in Russia harbouring varying degrees of expectation for the tournament, from the realism of Papua New Guinea to the cautious optimism of Uruguay and trophy holders Romania.

Italian captain Tommaso Benvenuti, a dashing outside centre with Benetton Treviso, was one of 14 veterans of the 2009 Junior World Championship in Japan, at the end of which Italy, together with Uruguay, Canada and hosts Japan, were relegated to the JWRT as the number of participants in JWC was reduced from 16 to 12. The experience of the squad, as well the expertise acquired during the high-intensity Under 20 Six Nations Championship, made the Italians one of the tournament's favourites alongside Canada and Japan.

In the end Italy lived up to their pre-tournament-favourites tag by defeating Japan 36-7 in a one-sided final at the Slava Stadium. Skipper Benvenuti scored a try after a couple of minutes, with Antonio Denti adding a second within ten minutes of kick-off. Two further tries from Michele Mortali and Gabriele Cicchinelli put the match beyond the reach of the Japanese, who nevertheless scored a consolation try through Mao Enoki. Italy had secured their place in the final in dramatic circumstances, Japanese referee Akihisa Aso awarding them a late penalty try against Uruguay in the eighth minute of time added on; the final score was 16-12. Although held to a 20-20 draw by a lively and talented Zimbabwe team, Japan still reached the final, thanks to a comprehensive 38-17 defeat of Canada in round three.

While keen to return to the elite division, the Japanese seemed well aware of the developmental value of the tournament, as Japan manager Takashi Hasunuma explained before the tournament kicked off: 'Many of these boys will form the core of the Japan team who compete in the RWC 2019 in Japan. This is why this tournament is very important for us in so many ways.'

Russia made history by becoming the first side to win an international match in sudden-death. A penalty in extra time against Romania secured Stanislav Selskiy and his team-mates a 23-20 victory and the bronze medals. Russia, who had been lucky to win by two points 17-15 against Canada, managed again to scrape through by a similar margin, 21-19, against a lively and definitely out-of-luck Zimbabwe to finish in second place in their group. Meanwhile Uruguay edged out Canada

LEFT Papua New Guinea's Nigel Genia, brother of Wallaby scrum half Will Genia.

FACING PAGE Former Nigeria international Andrew Mama, flanked by his sons Dante and Marco, both of whom represented Zimbabwe Under 20.

13-11 with a last-minute penalty by Agustín Ormaechea to take fifth place, and Zimbabwe finished seventh with a 46-22 win over Papua New Guinea.

Indeed Zimbabwe were arguably the surprise of the tournament. There was a firm sense of rugby tradition in the young and talented side, with many of the players and members of the management team coming from strong rugby family backgrounds. Centre David Fussell's father Phillip played for Mashonaland, while Hamish Watson played centre for Rhodesia in the Craven Week in 1968 and 1969 – 40 years before son David, a lock forward with the Under 20s, played in Craven Week 2009. Sasha Holloway's father played flank forward for Old Miltonians and Matabeleland, while Rory McWade, father of utility back Jonathan McWade, is an international referee. Schalk Ferreira's father Jan Jacobus represented Mashonaland Country Districts and the Army, and Daniel Robertson's father played for the Banket club and Mashonaland Country Districts.

Bernard 'Buster' Rutter, father of flank forward Luke, played club and provincial rugby and captained both Old Hararians and Mashonaland Country Districts, while Peter Kaulback, father of skipper Graham Kaulback, played for Natal Under 20 and Mashonaland before representing Zimbabwe at the inaugural Rugby World Cup in 1987, where he enjoyed the rare distinction of scoring a try against the French. 'As a player and a father and former World Cup player, I am so incredibly proud to have a son who is also playing in a World Cup,' he said.

Andrew Mama, a former Nigeria international, was in Moscow following the fortunes of his sons Dante and Marco, two of the mainstays of the youthful Zimbabwe team. Both played in the Craven Week, and their athletic prowess earned them sports scholarships to Millfield School, where they played for the school and fine-tuned their rugby skills. Marco, a flanker who had to fly back to the UK to sit his A-level exams after the Japan match, has signed a professional contract with Bristol, while older brother Dante, in his second year at Loughborough University, regained both health and fitness just in time for the Moscow tournament after a season dogged by injury.

Rod says the mix of players with experience and youth is similar to the Brumbies, noting 'we also had to be successful early on. Although, in a lot of ways it is very different to the Brumbies because with the Brumbies we were on an even playing field, we were actually competing with the other clubs to sign up players.

'This time the majority of players are signed up so we have to bring in players from overseas. That's not necessarily a bad thing, it's just different; and we've got a lot of players who haven't played alongside each other before and that's something we're going to have to work on.'

One of the key challenges for the Rebels has been the restrictions around recruitment. An embargo was designed to prevent any aggressive recruiting destabilising the current four Australian Super teams. As compensation the Australian Rugby Union allowed the Rebels to contract up to ten foreign players.

'As a side we have to be successful from year one. We don't have the luxury of building over three years. We have to be very competitive so we have to have a lot of experienced players in the side. We will be mixing that with a blend of youth with the idea that in three years' time when some of the older players are retiring or leaving we will have a good base of young players coming through.

'We have more than ten captains in the side … that gives you an idea of the intellectual property we have from all over the world. We've got players like Stirling Mortlock and Gareth Delve who played for Wales and is the captain of Gloucester, Michael Lipman who played for England and is captain of Warringah. Those sorts of players bring a great deal of leadership to the side. I will look to them to help develop the side that will be playing so I would hope from the time we come together

in October to running out in February we will have a unique style to Melbourne. One of our first signings was Danny Cipriani and it's going to be interesting to see how he evolves into southern hemisphere-type rugby. He has made some huge sacrifices in coming over, he said he missed out on the English squad because he is coming to the Rebels. It's great he is coming here for the right reasons, he wants to look at himself and his game and other ways of doing things so that's right up our alley.'

One of Macqueen's assistant coaches, Damien Hill, comes from the highly successful Sydney University club side in Sydney and he brings with him players from the club such as former Wallaby Al Campbell, former uni skipper Tim Davidson and promising youngster Laurie Weeks.

'One of the reasons I thought Damien would be good for the franchise is because of the culture they have built within Sydney Uni; so, I'm happy to have players out of there who bring some of that culture with them.

'We've been careful to select the type of players who will play the kind of game we want to play … we've been very particular.'

Macqueen has stayed true to a commitment he made not to poach Melbourne Storm rugby league players; but he has been on the lookout for talent to switch codes. Jarrod Saffy is the first National Rugby League (NRL) player to sign with the Rebels. He comes from the St George Illawarra Dragons league club. The back-rower does have a background in rugby union though, which will make the transition easier.

'I've got a simple philosophy that they are Australians and there are some very talented rugby league players and we need as much depth as possible so provided that they have the skill set they need for rugby union and the culture I think they're a great asset to us. I'm very optimistic about some of the values the league players will bring to us in terms of playing ability and attitude. They play week in, week out, very hard football and I don't think that's a bad thing for us to bring into this side.'

Macqueen hopes this mix of players will combine well when it's time to face some of the toughest provincial sides in the world; however, his broader and longer-term approach to building clubs means that he won't be measuring his success in terms of just winning and losing games, 'but I'm sure that's how we will be measured. From my perspective it's about doing everything as well as we can, having some very high standards in what we do and living and breathing those standards and I think if we do that success will follow.

'I'm really enjoying this challenge and my main ambition is to this see this through and if it's successful and Melbourne ends up with home-grown Wallabies I'll be very happy.'

Macqueen is innovative. He has always run his teams like a business.

In his message to the supporters on the Rebels website Macqueen says: 'It's not often you get the chance to start something from scratch; to create a new team and a new culture; to be the first representative side for a city. We, the Melbourne Rebels, have been afforded that opportunity and look forward to enjoying this special journey with you, our supporters.'

He is determined that his new side will develop a culture that is unique to Melbourne and the team's strip and song will reflect this. 'We are looking to develop a culture of humility within the side so I'd like to think that while we do things differently we are seen as a side with a very good culture … It's going to come from the players and the staff, together we've got some black-and-white guidelines … we're looking to be involved in the community and schools. Part of their tenure is our "Five Star Program". They will be an ambassador for club sides, schools and charities and businesses in Melbourne; so, they're going to start thinking about life after rugby early on. That balance in life I believe helps them to be better footballers and people so hopefully that will add to the culture.'

As part of this balance the Rebels will make a conscious effort to involve players' partners. 'We have many people coming into Melbourne, and quite a few from overseas, so that can amount to loneliness so we will have a special area designed to help out the partners and the families. We will help put them into good schools and have regular meetings and include them in the team's activities.'

The Rebels are the first privately owned professional rugby team in Australia. The club is run by a board chaired by the majority owner, media and communications millionaire Harold Mitchell. And while surprisingly Mitchell is not a rugby fanatic, he is passionate about anything he sees as good for the city of Melbourne. 'That's one of the reasons I decided to do this; because it is unique, particularly in Australia, to have private ownership [of a professional rugby team],' Macqueen explained. 'It makes it a lot easier because we don't have as much politics as the average side has, there's no baggage to be carried and quick decisions can be made. We've had some issues losing our CEO early and some issues around recruiting but we've been able to get on with it and make some quick decisions and move forward. They have been a good example in the difference in reaction time when you have private ownership.'

In January 2010 Brian Waldron, then CEO of the Melbourne Storm NRL club, was appointed inaugural chief executive of the Rebels. But this was to be a short-lived appointment. In April 2010 Waldron was implicated in the systemic breach of the NRL salary cap while at the Storm. It was a huge scandal in Australian sport and the Australian Premiership-winning side was stripped of two National Rugby League

BELOW The Rebels have signed some big-name players, such as Stirling Mortlock, seen here being chaired from the field after the Brumbies' final home match of the 2010 Super 14.

FACING PAGE Sometime England fly half Danny Cipriani is another heading for Melbourne for the 2011 Super 15.

titles (2007 and 2009) and fined A$1.6 million for salary-cap breaches. Waldron subsequently tendered his resignation from the Rebels and former NSW Waratahs and Manly Sea Eagles CEO Pat Wilson was immediately appointed interim CEO for the Melbourne club.

'I felt very sorry for Brian, it was one of those things, it was difficult at the time but I think from our perspective the board acted very well and very swiftly and we really just got on with it. That's in the past now … you're always going to have some tough times early on. It's all part and parcel of trying something new; so, while I won't say we expected it, they are the sort of things that happen.'

As a former Wallaby coach he is mature and sensible about his relationship with, and eventually his contribution through the Melbourne Rebels to, the national side. 'I think having been in that position myself I understand a lot of what Rob Deans's requirements will be. I think one of the things he would want us to do is get on with it and play innovative rugby.

'I think that's one of the beauties of the Super competition: that the different coaches can come up with new ideas and innovations; and when the Australian team comes together, the [national] coach is able to use a lot of those and put it into the mix of the Wallabies.

'I will be talking to Robbie on a regular basis and I will get feedback from him particularly on what he thinks of some of the players because from our perspective the more players we can get in the Wallabies the happier we will be.'

No matter how well the Rebels perform, Macqueen is clear that he won't accept a recall to the national role: 'I can promise I will not be interested in getting back involved with coaching the Wallabies. I've been there and done that. I'm sure that opportunity will be there for a younger person to get involved.'

His clarity of vision and sense of focus on this challenge is not surprising, as he has done it before; and if he is able to emulate his previous success, Australian rugby will be the winner.

A Promising Start
Andy Robinson and Scotland
by ALAN LORIMER

'Players at Edinburgh, where Robinson had a successful and rehabilitating two-year spell after his dismissal from the England job, have spoken of his attention to detail'

Twelve months after succeeding Frank Hadden, Scotland's coach Andy Robinson was able to look back with more than a degree of satisfaction on his first year in charge of the national team, a year that concluded with a double success on the Scots' two-Test tour to Argentina last summer. Overall Robinson achieved a more than 50 per cent success rate from the ten matches Scotland played under his direction, with wins over Fiji, Australia and Ireland adding to the two victories on the summer tour of Argentina. The Pumas, however, dished up one of Robinson's four defeats when they won 9-6 at Murrayfield in November of last year, the other reverses being against France, Wales and, most disastrously, Italy.

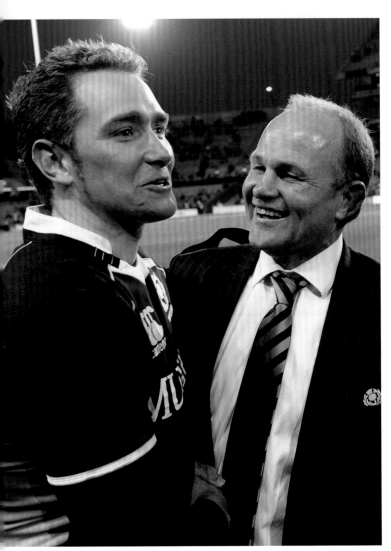

Then of course there was that emotionally difficult game against England at Murrayfield, potentially the hardest for former Bath player Robinson. In the event the Calcutta Cup match followed the pattern of recent meetings at Murrayfield between these old foes, ending in a dull draw. All of which meant that Robinson finished his first year at the helm with more victories than defeats but enough of the latter to avoid any sense of complacency.

Speaking after his side's win over Argentina in the Second Test at Mar del Plata, Robinson refused to indulge in triumphalism, instead striking a realistic and cautionary note. 'If we stand still we'll lose. We won these games by small margins and we have a long, long way to go. If we don't improve we'll get blown away in the autumn Tests and the Six Nations.

'From here it gets harder for the players. They have set themselves some standards and they have to live up to them,' said Robinson, whose side will face Argentina again when the Scots play the Pumas in the pool stages of the 2011 Rugby World Cup in New Zealand.

For Robinson to achieve the desired improvement will be a difficult task. The former England player and coach has a critically small pool of players from which to choose his squad – exacerbated by the decision three years ago to cull the Borders team – and that will always limit his ambitions.

Nor, unlike England and to a lesser extent Wales, is there the conveyor belt of young talent pouring out of the professional academies on to the rugby market annually north of the border. Indeed Scotland has only a handful of youngsters who are attached to academies, but while that affects the Scots' ability to compete seriously in the likes of the Junior World Championship, it does remove the disappointment that inevitably follows post-apprenticeship rejection. That situation may improve, but only marginally, through the influence of New Zealander Graham Lowe, Scotland's new performance director.

Lowe has identified ways of improving Scottish rugby, some of which – Sevens, for example – could impact on the senior side. In the shorter term, though, Robinson will have to work with what he has in front of him. But he has already effected a harder edge to the Scotland pack, he has recruited Gregor Townsend as backs mentor and has the steadying influence of fellow Englishman Graham Steadman as defence coach.

What remains a big challenge is creating a back division that can nail scoring opportunities and show creativity and vision. Robinson desperately needs what in the southern hemisphere they term a 'second five-eighth', a player who can offer the running and kicking skills of a fly half and has the strength to cope with the demands of the centre position. The choices, however, in the Scottish game are few.

He may also require to dig out another fly half. Dan Parks will be the obvious choice for the World Cup, but given the casualty rate last season among Scotland's top backs it would be better to have a Plan B. That may require taking a gamble on young fly halves from Edinburgh and Glasgow and even promoting from the Sevens squad.

Players at Edinburgh, where Robinson had a successful and rehabilitating two-year spell after his dismissal from the England job, have spoken of his attention to detail, of his understanding of the game situation, of his sheer candour and of his ability to work with

FACING PAGE The good times. Andy Robinson congratulates fly half Dan Parks after Scotland's 23-20 Six Nations victory over Ireland in Dublin in March.

ABOVE ... And the bad. Robinson and attack coach Gregor Townsend look on in Rome as Scotland go down to Italy.

FOLLOWING PAGE, TOP Australia's Mark Chisholm takes the ball into contact in the autumn 2009 match at Murrayfield, but (**BOTTOM**) it was Scotland's day to celebrate, having recorded a 9-8 win.

all of his players. These assets will be equally valuable at national level, but perhaps just as important is the way that rugby north of the border has accepted and welcomed Robinson into the Scotland fold.

England may have said no, but Scotland have said yes to a coach in whom the rugby fraternity has faith. But while the first year has been a relative success for Robinson, it is the next phase and in particular the World Cup that will be the real test.

New Zealand Awaits
the RWC 2011 Qualifying Process

by CHRIS THAU

'In Europe the qualifying process started with the match between Slovenia and Hungary in Ljubljana in September 2008 and ended six rounds and 93 matches later'

RWC 2011 kicks off on 9 September 2011 with the match between hosts New Zealand and Tonga at Eden Park in Auckland and will end on 23 October with the final at the same venue. In between there will be a further 47 matches – 31 in the pools and 15 in the knockout stage – at 11 venues throughout New Zealand. By the autumn of 2010, the 20-nation tournament line-up was only two matches away from completion; all that remained was the home-and-away Repechage final between Uruguay and Romania in November. The final act of the qualifying process will provide an intriguing contest between Los Teros, coached by former Puma Gonzalo Camardón, and the Romanians, under the joint Romanian/New Zealand management of Romeo Gontineac and Steve McDowall. The winner of the two-leg final will join Argentina, England, Scotland and European qualifying zone winners Georgia in Pool B of RWC 2011.

ABOVE Romania flanker and skipper Stelian Burcea in action during the 56-13 defeat of Tunisia in the Repechage semi-final at Buzau.

in the Olympics was in 1924 in Paris when the USA won the gold medal. That was a 15-a-side competition; in Rio the rugby will be Sevens.

A great deal of the credit for rugby once again becoming an Olympic sport must go to the Cathay Pacific Sevens tournament. The Hong Kong Sevens appeared on the radar of the Olympic Committee over ten years ago when the IRB Rugby World Cup Sevens was staged at the Hong Kong Stadium, and although it failed to win approval for the Olympics in Beijing or London, regular monitoring of the situation eventually secured the ultimate prize for Rio in 2016. The RWC Sevens was a big success in Dubai in 2009 and the IRB Sevens World Series was also very popular in 2009-10, but now the world's top Sevens players will all be chasing a glittering new target – an Olympic gold medal.

As we know from the results of decades of the Cathay Pacific tournament, Sevens is not always dominated by the giants of the game. Yes, England, New Zealand and Australia do very well, but so too do teams like Samoa and Fiji. Sevens suits them perfectly. And other lesser lights of 15-man rugby use the platform of the Sevens game to parade their talent. In Hong Kong in 2010 Kenya lost narrowly, 21-12, to mighty New Zealand in the Cup quarter-finals, having actually beaten the Kiwis at the same stage in 2009. Six Nations teams were also involved in results which would not have happened in 15-a-side rugby – Wales lost to Hong Kong 21-19, while Italy lost 26-19 to the same opposition in the Shield semi-finals, and France lost to Portugal 17-7 in the quarter-finals of the Bowl. That is the fascination of Sevens and why the Cathay Pacific Hong Kong Sevens of 2010 was a sell-out tournament (see pages 56-57 for shots of this year's crowd).

Meanwhile, in the Cup competition no one could overcome the force of the South Sea islanders of Samoa, who ultimately proved too strong for all-comers, including England, whom they beat 28-24 in the semi-finals, and New Zealand, whom they met in the final. In the latter match, Kurt Baker scored twice to rocket the Kiwis to an early 14-0 lead. Baker was this year's Cathay Pacific Hong Kong tournament top scorer with 61 points including nine tries.

However, Stephen Betham's side showed huge composure and battling qualities to hit back. Simaika Mikaele scored twice before the break to cut the deficit to two points, and with Baker in the sin-bin for a late tackle, Mikaele Pesamino scored after the break to put the Samoans ahead. The leading scorer in the 2009-10 IRB Sevens World Series then touched down again to put the game beyond New Zealand, who managed a late consolation try through Toby Arnold.

The Samoans had been the first team through to the Cup final after defeating the USA 24-7 in the quarters and then winning that pulsating semi-final against England, which saw Ben Ryan's men spurred on by a passionate expat crowd to take Samoa down to the wire. New Zealand had qualified with the victory against Kenya mentioned earlier and a 33-28 win over Fiji in the semis.

In the other competitions, Australia beat the 2009 IRB Sevens World Series champions South Africa to win the Plate. Robbie Coleman scored two tries, one in each half, to inspire the Wallaby Seven to a 12-5 victory over the Boks, for whom Sampie Mastriet scored the only try.

Earlier, both sides had lost closely in their respective Cup quarter-finals – Australia 26-19 against England at the death and South Africa 14-12 against Fiji – but they recovered well to beat USA and Kenya, 21-12 and 19-12 respectively, in the Plate semis to reach the final.

In the Bowl final Canada scored five tries to Wales's three to clinch the title. Morgan Williams' side had beaten Tonga 26-0 in the Bowl quarter-finals and then edged Portugal 26-24 in the semis, before getting the better of the Welsh.

Finally Hong Kong delighted the home crowd by winning all three of their games on the final day to capture the Shield title, collecting their first silverware on home soil for nine years. Dai Rees's team saw off local rivals Korea 31-14 in the Shield quarters and then Italy in the semi-finals, before producing a sparkling performance to beat Russia 19-17 in the final. Rowan Varty was top scorer for the home side with six tries over the three days.

Roll on the Hong Kong Sevens every year, and roll on the Olympics in 2016.

"THE DEPTH OF FLYING EXPERIENCE IN OUR TEAM IS REMARKABLE."

Evan Summerfield, Senior Captain
Cathay Pacific Airways

Like many of our pilots, Evan had years of flying experience even before he joined us. Meet Evan and other members of the Cathay Pacific team at www.cathaypacific.com. And while you're there, check out our great fares to over 110 destinations worldwide* – and if you meet Evan, maybe he'll tell you about his adventures in the Australian Outback.

Great service. Great people. Great fares. Visit cathaypacific.com

   Serving the UK for 30 years

DRAGONAIR

* Includes codeshare services.

CATHAY PACIFIC

Summer Tours 2010
England Down Under

by CHRIS FOY

'Northampton's rangy, bone-crunching Courtney Lawes carried and tackled with staggering ferocity and the hosts simply couldn't contain him'

It is too early to be sure, but in time England's 2010 trip Down Under may come to be regarded as a watershed for Martin Johnson and his embattled coaches – the period when a corner was finally turned. The mood within the Red Rose squad was utterly transformed on a remarkable night in Sydney, when the tourists rallied from their First Test defeat in Perth to beat Australia. They did so by just a single point, but that narrowest of margins was enough to give credibility and breathing space to a previously struggling regime.

Following another grim Six Nations campaign, this five-match crusade in Australia and New Zealand had loomed as a potentially punishing ordeal for an England team still lacking clarity of selection and tactical direction. The inclusion of two midweek matches against the Australian Barbarians and one against New Zealand Maori gave this the feel of a proper old-school tour and one which would offer no hiding places.

Johnson's decision to take an expanded 44-man playing party to cope with the busy schedule presented a danger in itself. The manager was adamant that there would be ample game time for one and all, but that left him juggling the twin targets of results and development. Experimenting and winning do not often go hand in hand in hostile territory south of the equator, but in the event a reasonable balance was struck.

When the dust had settled after the Maori match, which served as the tour finale, all but four players had featured in one starting XV or another. The unlucky quartet who made up the numbers were Shane Geraghty, Paul Hodgson, Rob Webber and a certain Mr J. Wilkinson, who had to settle for acting as Toby Flood's understudy. Yet the rotation system didn't obviously hamper England along the way. They finished up with a return of two wins, one draw and two defeats, and privately Johnson would surely have settled for that scenario before departure at the end of May.

Perhaps the most encouraging aspect of the exercise for the former national captain was the evidence of an emerging younger generation who may just give England the power, cutting edge and youthful verve to make an impact at next year's World Cup. Several tyros stood tall, none more so than Dan Cole.

The Leicester prop confirmed his status as the find of the season by leading the scrummaging rout of the Wallabies in Perth, which earned the visitors two penalty tries and very nearly snatched a shock win. Australia were without four leading front-row forwards, and coach Robbie Deans was forced to watch his supporting cast being annihilated.

Steve Thompson, England's World Cup-winning hooker, referred to the quietly menacing Cole as a 'serial killer', which the local media latched on to as a suitably dread-inspiring moniker for their

ABOVE England hooker Steve Thompson and the 'quietly menacing' Dan Cole prepare to pack down against the Wallabies in the Second Test.

FACING PAGE Ben Youngs scoots over for England's first try in their 21-20 victory at Sydney.

ABOVE Full back Ben Foden takes a high ball ahead of Australia's Adam Ashley-Cooper in Sydney. Foden was very much part of England's 'outbreak of adventure' in the Second Test.

FACING PAGE Midweek skipper Chris Robshaw runs at New Zealand Maori. There was more adventure from England in Napier, but too many missed tackles in the 35-28 defeat.

team's tormentor. The tight-head finished the Sydney Test with a bloodied, bandaged head and horribly swollen black eye, which served to enhance an increasingly fearsome image.

There were several other rookies who stood out. Gloucester lock Dave Attwood showcased his Johnson-like abrasive qualities in the midweek side, turning in a stirring performance in the 15-9 win against the Barbarians in Gosford. He was fortunate to still be around at that stage after a stamping charge against him from the previous week was dropped on a technicality, but he certainly made the most of his reprieve to earn a place in the senior Elite Player Squad ranks.

Another second-row came to the fore in Sydney. Northampton's rangy, bone-crunching Courtney Lawes played a sensational hand in the victory over the Wallabies after being drafted in to replace Simon Shaw. The 21-year-old carried and tackled with staggering ferocity and the hosts simply couldn't contain him. Lawes was making his starting debut, as was Ben Youngs, and the Leicester scrum half marked the occasion with a scorching, opportunist's try. Spying a gap from a line out, he darted into space and left Drew Mitchell clutching his vapour trail to score. It was the high point of a display full of pace and precision and commendable composure from such an inexperienced player.

That night, 19 June, was a red-letter occasion for England. Their 21-20 victory was only the third time they had beaten Australia away from home and was their first Test win in the southern hemisphere since the 2003 World Cup final. There was a parallel of sorts as it was a Wilkinson kick which ultimately clinched the win, but the match was most notable for a sudden resurgence of the

Red Rose attacking game. It came out of the blue. England had been stilted and tense in Perth, where there was an overreliance on the scrum which could not prevent the Wallabies from securing a 27-17 win. Then in Gosford they beat a poor Barbarians side by once again dominating the set-piece, grinding and kicking. But in the Second Test there was an encouraging outbreak of adventure.

Chris Ashton scored England's other try, but they could have had more, as Ben Foden danced, bobbed and weaved to create openings, and Shontayne Hape recovered from a poor debut seven days earlier to unlock doors in midfield with powerful running and offloading. Up front, Tom Croft looked like a Lion again as he rampaged around close enough to the contact areas to make a significant impact. Equally important was the robust, energetic defensive work, which nullified the threat posed by Quade Cooper, who had ripped England to pieces in Perth. Mike Ford, the defence coach, earned deserved plaudits for the planning which helped turn the tables, but he was often let down on the tour as too many individual tackles were missed. Saracens wing David Strettle will be haunted by his tame lapses against the Maori.

That final game proved to be something of a comedown for England, even though there were further glimpses of a renewed attacking spark which brought three more tries. The tourists played their part in a scintillating contest, but that was no consolation to Johnson, who was left seething by his team's inability to stop the powerful Maori backs running amok. If there was a consolation in a game which saw England surrender a 28-17 half-time lead to lose 35-28, it was the exhibition of fly-half craftsmanship by Charlie Hodgson. In his third starting appearance of the tour, the Sale No. 10 confirmed his dramatic re-emergence as a viable Test candidate.

Despite the defeat in Napier, Johnson insisted the overall tone was upbeat and on this occasion his positivity had substance. While Europe's finest endured yet more June gloom at the hands of the SANZAR heavyweights, England alone struck a telling blow for the north. That landmark win in Sydney prompted a greater sense of belief within the management ranks, which should permeate through to the players. And with Lewis Moody placing an iron grip on the captaincy with his demented heroics in the Second Test, the squad returned home with more stability – and depth – than when they left. So optimism was justified, but whether this was a welcome blip or the start of a sustained revival would become clear by the end of November.

Scotland in Argentina

by ALAN LORIMER

'Whether Scotland can carry this winning form forward remains to be seen, but certainly there is the impression that under Andy Robinson, they are beginning to gel as a team'

ABOVE Scotland celebrate their series win in Argentina after the Second Test at Mar del Plata.

Whatever the impact the results of Scotland's 2010 summer tour to Argentina eventually have on the game north of the border, the immediate effect was a hurried readjusting of the records by rugby historians to display a new and satisfying set of statistics. The two-Test series win was the first time that Scotland had completed an overseas tour to the southern hemisphere unbeaten, and with the Scots having won their final Six Nations Championship match against Ireland in Dublin it also was the first time that Scotland had won three consecutive away games since their Grand Slam year of 1984.

Arguably the greatest achievement was dismantling the hitherto impregnable fortress that was Tucumán, the 'wild west' outpost of Argentine rugby that has been the graveyard of numerous touring teams since 1973. For Scotland it was the chosen venue for the First Test against the Pumas, and as such, history was not on the side of the Scots. It seemed a self-fulfilling prophecy as Argentina led 13-6 midway through the first half with a try by centre Gonzalo Tiesi, from turnover ball and swift distribution, and a second touchdown, this time from flanker Juan Manuel Leguizamón from a perfectly placed cross-kick by fly half Felipe Contepomi. Scotland, who had won an unconvincing warm-up game at Murrayfield against an understrength Japan side, looked nervous and error-prone. But crucially they were playing expansive rugby, moving the ball wide and stretching the Puma back-line defence.

The try dividend for Scotland, however, was zero, but pressure produced points as Dan Parks kicked three first-half penalties and dropped a goal just before the break to leave his side within a point of the Pumas. And that was to be the theme of the second half. Scotland applied the pressure and Parks secured the points with three more penalty goals and a drop to steer the Scots to a 24-16 win and a place in Tucumán history as the first touring team to win a Test at the notorious ground.

It was then on to Mar del Plata for the Second Test. The coastal city, some 250 miles south of Buenos Aires, is something of a holiday resort in the summer, but in the winter its maritime position exposes it to some nasty weather off the Atlantic. Thus it was a wet welcome that greeted Scotland as unrelenting rain drenched the Test arena to make for difficult playing conditions, seemingly more likely to favour the heavier Puma pack. But a shock awaited the muscular Argentinians as Scotland struck within three minutes with a try by lock Jim Hamilton from close-range forward driving.

But that was to be the only try in a match that rapidly diminished as a spectacle as both sides opted for nothing too cavalier in the deteriorating conditions. But whereas the Argentine pack had looked the more powerful in the First Test, it was Scotland's front row who began to dominate the set-piece confrontation, with loose-head Allan Jacobsen and tight-head Moray Low emerging with full battle honours.

Although not as accurate with the boot in the Second Test, Parks was still able to provide the remainder of the points with the conversion of Hamilton's try and two penalty goals. Contepomi, before retiring injured, kicked two for the Pumas, and there was a third goal by Martín Rodríguez to take Argentina within four points. In a tense finale, Argentina had a late chance to overtake the Scots when they kicked to the corner from a penalty award. All that the Pumas seemingly had to do was gain possession from their own throw-in and then drive over the line. It was, however, not the script, as replacement lock Scott MacLeod, a basketball player before turning to rugby, soared into the air to steal the ball. It went back to replacement scrum half Mike Blair who hoofed the ball into the stands, leaving Scotland jubilant winners by 13-9 and Argentina in despair.

Quite apart from the lift in confidence that Scotland gained from their series win, there was also the matter of an upward shift for the Scots in the IRB rankings – timely, as it will affect the seedings for the 2011 World Cup. Whether Scotland can carry this winning

BELOW Moray Low takes on the Pumas as Scotland's pack get the upper hand at Mar del Plata.

FACING PAGE Scotland scrum half Rory Lawson looks outside to find Simon Danielli in support. Lawson started both Tests ahead of Mike Blair.

form forward remains to be seen, but certainly there is the impression that under Andy Robinson, Scotland are beginning to gel as a team. Crucially too, it is still by international standards a relatively young side that has yet to fully mature. That Scotland achieved success without Chris Paterson, Thom Evans, Rory Lamont, Euan Murray, Chris Cusiter and Nathan Hines was also laudable.

Robinson would certainly have applauded the Scotland forward pack in which a number of players came of age. Moray Low probably made the biggest advance, with powerful scrummaging against the one of the most feared front rows in Test rugby. He will now put pressure on Euan Murray, and with the Lions and Northampton prop subscribing to Sunday as a day of rest, and with Scotland playing two of their Six Nations matches on the Sabbath, Low, who is a useful ball player, could become the number one choice for the Scots.

Another player to emerge with an enhanced reputation was lock Al Kellock. The big Glasgow second-row took over the captaincy from the injured Chris Cusiter, and in the event led inspirationally. Behind Kellock, Glasgow's three Bs – Barclay, Beattie and Brown – again stood out, with Kelly Brown deserving most plaudits for his high work rate and clever use of the ball.

Behind the scrum there remains a question mark over Scotland's ability to score tries, but there were encouraging signs of incision from Nick de Luca and Max Evans, which suggests that Scotland's weakness of recent seasons could be remedied. One significant change that was achieved on tour was persuading Dan Parks to take the ball much flatter, in response to advice from backs coach Gregor Townsend. However much Parks changes his alignment, he will never be one of the truly great attacking fly halves, but with a prodigious boot he is a match winner; and provided he stays fit, Parks will be at the epicentre of Scotland's play in the 2011 World Cup. As if recognising this fact, Robinson deployed Parks for the full duration of both Tests, leaving Phil Godman as the only benchman not to have any game time.

Parks's half-back partner, Rory Lawson, took his chance to promote himself after confident displays in both Tests, suggesting that he may now have overtaken Blair in the pecking order. But whatever the rankings in the No. 9 position, it still means that Robinson has a luxury of choices at scrum half, a compensation, perhaps, for the lack of similar options in other areas of the team.

BEHIND SCOTTISH RUGBY.

Please enjoy our whisky responsibly.
for the facts drinkaware.co.uk

Wales in New Zealand

by GRAHAM CLUTTON

'For the optimists, the manner in which Warren Gatland's underpowered side finished the Second Test in Hamilton will have given some genuine reason for hope'

Y ou could have written the script long before Wales took to the field in Dunedin for what was to be the first of two more comprehensive defeats at the hands of New Zealand. Had you done so, it would have read something like this: 'Good start, early success giving way to errors and eventual defeat.' So, just as Wales had begun well against the Springboks in Cardiff on the eve of their two-match excursion Down Under, so they led in both Test matches against the All Blacks. Sadly, having capitulated in all too familiar fashion against the world champions on home soil on 5 June, so they fell to pieces on both occasions in New Zealand. At Carisbrook, in the final game to be played at the stadium, they squandered an early advantage before going down 42-9; seven days later in Hamilton, they were beaten 29-10 despite, once more, taking an early lead through the boot of Leigh Halfpenny.

For Wales coach Warren Gatland, whose return to New Zealand had been undertaken in hope

ABOVE Back-rower Rob McCusker of the Scarlets, in his third game for Wales, makes a break in Hamilton.

rather than expectation, it was a sobering conclusion to a season that began with genuine ambition and realistic hope. Without the resting Martyn Williams and the injured quartet of James Hook, Shane Williams, Gethin Jenkins and Luke Charteris, his squad lacked the necessary quality and composure to push an All Blacks side whose confidence had been slightly knocked in the second half against a 14-man Ireland side. In the end, it was a bridge too far on both occasions, with New Zealand, driven forward by the impeccable Dan Carter, extending their unbeaten stretch against Wales to 53 years.

For the optimists, the manner in which Gatland's underpowered side finished the Second Test in Hamilton will have given some genuine reason for hope. After all, a late try from Jamie Roberts after 15 minutes of concerted pressure in Kiwi territory suggested that Wales had at least grown in stature between the two games. 'It was a good way to finish although it would have been nice to have avoided conceding another try in injury time,' said Gatland, whose determination to establish greater strength in depth saw debuts on the tour for the Dragons wing Will Harries and Scarlets scrum half Tavis Knoyle. That pair, along with Tom Prydie, Dan Biggar, Craig Mitchell and Rob McCusker, featured heavily along the way, with Biggar winning the outside-half vote for the Second Test ahead of Stephen Jones.

For captain Ryan Jones, who was forced off in the Second Test with a bruised thigh, the emergence of so many gifted youngsters should be seen as a significant step in the right direction. Regardless of successive defeats, Jones firmly believes that Welsh rugby is in decent shape as the countdown to the World Cup begins in earnest. 'The tour provided a fantastic opportunity for the younger players like Dan Biggar and Tom Prydie,' said Jones. 'I spoke to Tom a few days before the Second Test and he said he had been a bit daunted going into the first game. However, he took a lot of confidence from that game, came through in one piece and will be all the better for the experience.

'The challenge for us is we have to create a belief in these youngsters that they believe, understand and can go into games with that confidence. We have seen the emergence of Dan Biggar, Andrew Bishop, Tom Prydie, Jon Davies, Will Harries, Craig Mitchell and Rob McCusker.

These are players who have earned that right and in getting the chance to tour New Zealand this far out from the World Cup, can only be of help to us.

'It makes the squad more competitive and there is a lot more for the players to play for next year. I honestly think we're in a good place. The standards are good and if we can keep this group of players together then we have a backbone. In the past we've always been regressing when we meet up for a new campaign, but as we speak, we are progressing.'

The one area in which Wales have developed out of all recognition in recent times is physicality. Once lambs to the slaughter against the southern hemisphere sides, the team has proved itself capable of achieving parity, at least, at the breakdown area. That improvement was clear for all to see in Dunedin where New Zealand struggled for long periods to establish the upper hand. In fact, it was not until Wales pressed the self-destruct button by turning over ball in key areas that the All Blacks wrested the initiative. After that, Carter kicked Wales into touch and victory became a formality for the hosts.

Jones said, 'I believe in the physicality and character of this team. We are big enough to compete in the set-piece and at the breakdown. I think we have reached a level where we can be competitive. That's the main foundation block for us. The players are fit enough and we can mix it with the best, but that's the minimum standard. We have to be technically and tactically more astute and do it for 80 minutes.

'When the momentum flow is against you, we have to weather the storm. We need to ask ourselves whether we can maintain our composure. Can we play our way out of it? That's where maturity and composure comes.'

Having shown that composure in the early stages of the First Test, Wales found themselves six points to the good, courtesy of a dropped goal from Stephen Jones and a Halfpenny penalty. Thereafter it was the mistakes that have driven Gatland to distraction this season that put paid to any chance of a first ever win on Kiwi soil. Keven Mealamu, Cory Jane, an inspired Carter (two) and Richard Kahui all crossed for tries, with Carter adding 17 points with the boot to finish with a personal haul of 27 points.

'We were missing players, but we caused New Zealand problems,' said Jones. 'I think we learned the importance of being physically and mentally tough and being accurate technically and tactically when it counts. You only get that by playing under this duress and pressure. That is exactly what the players experienced in Dunedin.'

Seven days later, Halfpenny's long-range penalty gave Wales a 3-0 lead in the Second Test at the Waikato Stadium. However, after that, New Zealand scored 22 unanswered points to set up a straightforward success. Roberts' late try was reward for some honest endeavour, but it was the All Blacks who had the final say when replacement outside half Aaron Cruden helped himself to a try in stoppage time.

Jones concluded, 'Playing South Africa before coming out here was tough as well, but the difficulty of this tour has been playing New Zealand in back-to-back weeks. That's tough. In the autumn, you may have two games, but with a second-tier nation sandwiched in the middle.

'But playing the Springboks, then having a week off and then facing New Zealand twice has given the players a glimpse of what it requires to play at this level and how you pick yourself up, dust yourself down and move on. That's what we will face at the World Cup. This experience can only be positive for us.'

BELOW Jerome Kaino cannot prevent Jamie Roberts' late score at Hamilton.

It will be back to New Zealand for that World Cup in 15 months' time, and back to Hamilton, where Wales play two group matches at the Waikato Stadium. By then, Gatland will hope to have ironed out the rough spots and put Wales in a position in which they can compete, for 80 minutes, against the best in the world. That's the challenge.

Ireland Down Under

by SEAN DIFFLEY

'Against New Zealand Maori, the back row of Chris Henry, Niall Ronan and the remarkable teenager Rhys Ruddock were outstanding, as was Geordan Murphy at full back'

It was a Down Under tour that appeared pretty much a disaster – three losses consisting of a record 66-28 nine-try horror defeat to New Zealand in New Plymouth; a decent enough revival against the centenary-celebrating Maori in their own Rotorua, before going under 31-28; and a 22-15 reverse to the Australians in Brisbane. It was 31 years since Ireland had won an away match against a southern hemisphere team, the kicking of Ollie Campbell having engineered no less than two Test victories over Australia in Brisbane and Sydney in 1979. Indeed the 2010 tour included the 24th successive loss to the Big Three below the equator. Ireland were not happy campers, and coach Declan Kidney was far from his happy self, with the 2009 Grand Slam memories now transformed into five successive defeats.

> **BELOW** Rob Kearney and Shane Jennings fail to prevent Jimmy Cowan from scoring the fifth of New Zealand's nine tries in the Test at New Plymouth.

Strangely enough, it was not quite the unsuccessful tour the statistics suggested. There was a fair amount of debate about the advisability of such a tour at the end of a busy home season. And in addition there were a quite remarkable number of 'unavailables' through injuries, which meant that Kidney was faced with building a squad without 14 of his obvious contingent, 14 who had played in the previous nine Tests over the 2009-10 season. Five of those who played against Australia had played in the winning Ireland A Churchill Cup side just 12 months before. And 19-year-old Rhys Ruddock – son of former Wales coach Mike Ruddock, who had declared for Ireland – was summoned to join the party from the Irish Under 20 team, which he was skippering at the Junior World Championship in Argentina. He played against the Maori and gained his first full Irish cap when he came on as a replacement against the Wallabies.

So the tourists were really an Irish B team and certainly hardly performed beyond that level against the All Blacks. That first half in New Plymouth against New Zealand was, without argument, the worst display by an Irish team, ever, in particular that horrible ten minutes in which Jamie Heaslip got his marching orders for the quaint use of his knees in a ruck and Ronan O'Gara got ten minutes in the bin, leaving just 13 green-clad players to face the mighty All Blacks. During that spate of Irish courtesy, New Zealand scored 21 points and the match was virtually over.

The curious aspect of the second half of the match was that the deflated Irish, with their complement of 14 players, managed to score four tries, one each from Brian O'Driscoll, Tommy Bowe, Gordon D'Arcy and debutant Dan Tuohy. The lock came on as a replacement and promptly trotted over from a ruck. O'Gara converted three of the tries, and Jonathan Sexton, who replaced O'Gara, knocked over the other. It's a fascinating thought, isn't it? Four tries in 40 minutes against

the All Blacks. Poirot might have the answer. The All Blacks certainly hadn't lost interest, and scoring nine tries (seven converted by their highly skilful out-half, Dan Carter, in between probing the Irish defence) is hardly a stamina-sapping operation compared with defending. The coaches on both sides will view the videos with renewed interest.

Perhaps the Irish weren't as bad as the All Blacks adventure suggested. There was a definite improvement against the Maori and the Wallabies, and both games could have been won. Once again the Irish started badly against the Maori, who went into an 18-3 lead, only for the tourists to hit back to lead 25-18; but it was 31-28 for the exultant Maori at the end. The back row of Chris Henry, Niall Ronan and the remarkable teenager Rhys Ruddock were outstanding, as was Geordan Murphy at full back for Rob Kearney, and Jonathan Sexton pulled the strings impressively at fly half.

There was renewed optimism when the party flew to Brisbane, with Sexton, who was to finish the tour with 14 successful place-kicks out of 15 attempts, the choice at fly half over O'Gara. Sexton kicked all Ireland's 15 points in Brisbane, but in a match that contained too many errors from both sides, Australia pierced the Irish defence for two tries that made all the difference in that 22-15 Wallaby victory. Even so, after shipping those 66 points just two weeks previously, the outcome for Ireland wasn't too shabby. Luke Burgess, the Australia scrum half, scored the first try for the home team, but the one flash of class came from out-half Quade Cooper, who with a quality bit of side-stepping eluded the midfield defence for a try on the stroke of half-time.

So, Irish hopes for the World Cup? After that flop against the All Blacks the Irish future looked bleak indeed. But the recovery was positive enough and several younger players, unconsidered until the spate of injuries gained them their chances, indicated that the new generation is promising. Players who showed up well on the tour include the teenage flanker Ruddock, wing Andrew Trimble, hooker Sean Cronin and lock Dan Tuohy. The emphasis for Declan Kidney in the new season is priming that lot and a few others with a bit more experience. The future is far from as desperate as that nine-try extravaganza in New Plymouth would imply.

Churchill Cup

by HUGH GODWIN

'The stand-in captain George Skivington was wreathed in smiles at the conclusion of an eclectic fortnight's competition which included teams from France, Russia and Uruguay'

The gleaming Red Bull Arena in Harrison, New Jersey, became the sixth different venue to stage a final of the annual Churchill Cup since its inception in 2003, and the celebrations were all white as England Saxons reclaimed the trophy. It was probably not the Saxons' finest hour, as their vanquished opponents – Russia and the USA in the pool phase and Canada on finals day at the newly built home of the local Major League Soccer franchise – were not as strong as some of

those in the past. But any international tournament victory is to be savoured and the stand-in captain George Skivington was wreathed in smiles at the conclusion of an eclectic fortnight's competition which included teams from France, Russia and Uruguay for the first time.

The six pool matches, as in 2009, were played across three days of double-headers at Infinity Park in the self-styled 'Rugbytown USA' of Glendale on the outskirts of Denver, Colorado. At their conclusion England were on top of Pool A but had waved their original skipper Phil Dowson and centre Brad Barritt off to the senior side's tour of Australia and New Zealand. Thus the theoretically second-string Saxons arrived at the 25,000-capacity Red Bull Arena – it was about a quarter full for the finals of Cup, Plate and Bowl – with the next best Englishmen after the top 46 (and a couple more absent injured). Churchill Cup final crowds have yet to crack five figures, but the Cup and Plate were broadcast to 63 million US homes by Universal Sports, in addition to Sky's customary live coverage of the whole competition in the UK. And the 'buddy' partnership between co-organisers England, the United States and Canada is going strong with a little help from the International Rugby Board, who set great store by tournament play as a means of developing the second- and third-tier unions.

The Saxons' rejigged coaching team of Stuart Lancaster (who had presided over the disappointing 2009 final defeat to Ireland A), Andy Farrell and Simon Hardy also had a stroke of luck

in avoiding France A in the Cup final. The French were expected to win Pool B with a strong squad drawn from nine clubs in their domestic league, but they were defeated 33-27 by Canada on the concluding day of pool play in the best match of the tournament. The French had already cantered past Uruguay 43-10, with Racing Métro fly half Jonathan Wisniewski pulling the strings. The South Americans were missing a handful of European-based players and had succumbed weakly to Canada, 48-6, after flanker Chauncey O'Toole ran in the first try from a shortened line out with telling ease.

Against Canada, who had enjoyed a week's rest compared with three days for their opponents, the French paired the Test No. 10 Lionel Beauxis with former Leicester scrum half Julien Dupuy and led 16-10 at half-time. But the soon to be Newport Gwent Dragons full back Matt Evans had shown Canada's quality with a clever grubber to make a try for No. 8 Aaron Carpenter, one of a quartet from English Championship clubs. And though the French must have had fleas in their ears from their coaches and former international stars Fabien Pelous and Olivier Magne, they could not keep the Canadians at bay. In the second half a try by Yoan Audrin and two Beauxis penalties were overhauled ultimately by a 71st-minute try for Canada by Brian Erichsen after flanker Adam Kleeberger intercepted a pass from the wing Julien Arias and wove upfield.

The Russians made their Churchill Cup debut against the USA in the Pool A opener, which was a rehearsal for their meeting at the 2011 World Cup, and unleashed the Sevens expert Vasily Artemyev for an 11th-minute try with a lovely break and chip over Chris Wyles, the USA's

LEFT Lee Dickson breaks for England Saxons against the USA during the pool game at Infinity Park, won 32-9 by the Saxons.

Saracens full back. A try from another of the competition's outstanding personalities, back-rower Victor Gresev, put Russia 15-14 ahead at the interval. The USA eventually pulled through 39-22, helped by a try with a side-step and turbo-boosted run from their best-known player, the Biarritz wing Takudzwa 'Zee' Ngwenya. 'It's an adjustment to come back to the US team and we're just trying to keep it going and show the boys a different level,' said Ngwenya.

Russia found the Saxons to be operating on a higher plane, although Artemyev, the right wing who moulded his game while studying in Dublin, burst through England's 10–12 channel for a morale-boosting try just before half-time. England led 28-14 at the break, and 49-17 by the end after accumulating seven tries including two by Tom Varndell. The Wasps wing repeated that feat against the USA, when the champions-to-be raced to an 18-3 lead in 15 minutes and won 32-9. Alex Goode, in a selection agreed with the senior team's manager Martin Johnson, showed flashes of the talent at fly half his club Saracens are expected to nurture next season.

As the six teams moved east for finals day, the Saxons restored Goode to full back, which meant Nick Abendanon of Bath, in his fourth successive Churchill Cup, and Gloucester's James Simpson-Daniel, a veteran of the 2003 final won by England A as they were then, occupied the wings. Skivington and James Hudson locked a scrum which was not huge by some English standards but had the promising London Irish prop Alex Corbisiero anxious to impress. 'Obviously the English teams try to outmuscle you and our scrum's going to be in for a big day,' predicted Canada's New Zealander coach, Kieran Crowley, and he was spot on.

As they had in the pool matches, the Saxons scored comfortably early. Stephen Myler, the fly half who would go on to land seven kicks out of seven before missing with his final conversion attempt, popped over a penalty after three minutes. Then a line out 30 metres from the Canadian line was tapped back by No. 8 Luke Narraway with help from his loose-head prop Nick Wood, and Lee Dickson – Myler's Northampton clubmate and half-back partner – made a couple of metres followed in kind by flankers Andy Saull and Tom Wood. From there, Dickson and Myler spread the play wide, and while another Saint, Jon Clarke, ran a decoy, his fellow centre Anthony Allen and Goode fed Abendanon, who stepped off his left foot to get past Canada full back James Pritchard and dotted down neatly despite the attentions of two tacklers. It was a fine team try.

The scrum was the source of the Saxons' next try, finished at pace by Goode, and England led 17-0, which became 23-13 by the interval, though Canada rued three missed goal kicks. They also missed the control at fly half of Ander Monro, waylaid by a gall-bladder complaint. Assistant Coach Farrell – another man of Saracens – called on the Saxons to 'lift the intensity for the next 10 minutes and keep it there', and for the third quarter at least in 80-degree heat they complied. Myler kicked his fourth penalty and converted a 46th-minute try for Clarke at the end of a beautiful touch-line counterattack by Goode and Abendanon from the latter's quickly taken line out. Trailing 33-13, Canada were in catch-up mode, kicking penalties to touch and so on. A sweeping move right to left, then back again, finished with Narraway scoring from a long pass by Clarke and a short one by replacement lock Graham Kitchener. Canada had the last try, by replacement Ryan Smith, but it was a clear-cut result, 38-18. The dashing Abendanon was named man of the tournament and put the Saxons' victory down to superior fitness thanks to an immediate transition from the domestic season.

The French swallowed their pride to prevail in the Plate final, 24-10, against the USA, with Beauxis converting three tries and adding a penalty. And the well-organised Russians – 12 of their starting XV hailed from the champion club, VVA-Podmoskovje – collected the Bowl with a 38-19 defeat of the disappointing Uruguayans in which Artemyev scored for the third match running.

The 2011 competition may be relocated again to England, as it was in the World Cup year of 2007. For the time being the Saxons could gaze at the Manhattan skyline from their New York hotel and conclude they had comfortably scaled the heights required to capture their fifth Churchill Cup title in eight attempts.

33°S – Sydney, Australia

Who helps you get more from your game?

With HSBC Premier, you'll enjoy free membership to our HSBC Premier Golf Network. This exclusive service provides players of all abilities with preferential access to some of the best courses in Britain.

Our fantastic green fees, exclusive offers and bespoke lesson packages with PGA Pros will help you get the most out of this great game. Plus, you'll receive a monthly newsletter packed full of features, tips from the Pros and equipment reviews to keep you informed.

To discover more about HSBC Premier, visit hsbc.co.uk/premier or your local branch. Or call us on 0800 432 0576.

To find out about our Premier Golf Network, visit www.hsbc.co.uk/premier-golf-network.

HSBC Premier Golf Network | **HSBC** The world's local bank

HOME FRONT

Proving Critics Wrong
Saracens Under Brendan Venter

by **CHRIS JONES**

'Venter operated a rota system for his players until the final couple of games and instead of splitting the camp, it proved to be a key factor in getting Sarries to the final'

Brendan Venter promised to make an impact with his Saracens squad last season and achieved that on and off the pitch, taking the club into a first Guinness Premiership final – a game he had to watch at home after being banned for ten weeks by a Rugby Football Union disciplinary hearing. Venter, the Saracens director of rugby, was initially banned for 14 weeks for 'provocative and inappropriate gestures and comments' aimed at Leicester fans at Welford Road at the end of the regular season. At an appeal, the sanction was reduced to ten weeks, but the insistence that he was not to be at Twickenham for the final against Leicester remained. With the former Springbok centre watching with his son at home, Sarries came agonisingly close to winning the title for the first time in their professional history, losing 33-27, but there is no hiding from the fact that Venter and co. have created something special in North London.

RIGHT Director of rugby Brendan Venter (right) and first-team coach Mark McCall watch a training session at the Saracens training ground in St Albans.

FACING PAGE Brad Barritt scores for Saracens in their friendly against South Africa at Wembley in November 2009. Once an Emerging Springbok, Barritt is in the England Saxons squad and appeared for the full England side against New Zealand Maori in June 2010.

And they didn't restrict themselves to parading their rugby skills at Vicarage Road, taking over Wembley for four matches and winning all of them – including beating the Springboks – in front of average crowds of more than 40,000. It was a confirmation that Venter had been the right man to take over after Eddie Jones was forced out of the club.

Venter's remarkable debut campaign was born in Cape Town, where he took the squad for three pre-season warm-up games. Training was kept to a minimum around the games while off-the-field activities – braais and beers – were the order of the day, and this trip would be constantly mentioned by players as they explained how a new squad could gel so quickly and lead the Premiership at the turn of the year.

The club had lived with the tag of 'underachievers' ever since they won the Tetley's Bitter Cup in 1998 and absolutely nothing after that season, despite owner Nigel Wray spending millions to attract a host of coaches and big-name players. Venter knew what he was taking on and said on arrival about that tag: 'I am not sure we can shrug that off, but I don't lose one wink of sleep because I can't do anything about the baggage of the past – all I can do is go forward. This club needs stability after so many changes of coach in recent years [eight in seven years] and one of the reasons I didn't let Eddie Jones's coaching staff go is because they are great people and I have enjoyed working with them.

'When I took the job I explained that I expected to get results and this is not a three-year or five-year project. I don't think I am hard on myself and if things go wrong I move on and in my career as a doctor I have seen real things going wrong in people's lives and know about the bigger picture and I keep things in perspective.'

Initially, Venter kept the game plan simple, relying on the kicking game to get his team into enemy territory and then taking the points through the boots of either Glen Jackson (who has now retired to become a professional referee in New Zealand) or Derick Hougaard, who will vie with the mercurial England Saxons star Alex Goode for the No. 10 spot next season. When the referees changed the way they looked at the breakdown, Sarries changed tack and formulated a new, exciting way of playing after another beers-and-chat trip – this time to Brighton.

'The building blocks of our game were in place and with the change in interpretation by referees, which helped attacking rugby, we decided to play this way,' said Venter. 'Early in the season we weren't good enough even though we had been practising in pre-season to perform like this and that is why I am so excited about where we can take this club.

'Our vision is to win the Premiership and we want to achieve that target. Having lost to Leicester, we will just have to come back stronger as a club next season.'

Venter operated a rota system for his players until the final couple of games and instead of splitting the camp, it proved to be a key factor in getting Sarries to the final. Players knew they would be having a run of games and when that would happen, allowing them to spend time with family and even head to various parts of the world in their weeks off. Venter took time to head back to Cape Town to bring his family over for Christmas, and while the rest of the Premiership waited for the Sarries bubble to burst, the director of rugby kept on proving critics wrong.

Ernst Joubert, the No. 8, and goal-kicker Hougaard also went back to their native South Africa before Christmas for a short break in Cape Town, while Italy prop Matías Agüero was given ten days in Argentina visiting his relations; centre Kameli Ratuvou earned the highest number of air miles making the long trip home to Fiji to see his family in the run-up to Christmas. Venter explained: 'I wasn't in Castres for our game and the team was prepared brilliantly by Mark McCall, the head coach. I enjoyed the great win via a mobile put on speaker phone in the dressing room after the match and I was able to give the squad my congratulations and listen to their victory song.

'We had a very healthy situation with players knowing exactly where they stood and when they were playing and so they could plan ahead. There were absurd suggestions that we were going to make Sarries a South African club when, in fact, everyone has come here and embraced the Premiership and become part of English rugby.'

Last season, the club's critics claimed Sarries had become an outpost of South African rugby imposed upon the English game, and the surnames of many of the squad do point towards their African roots. The fact the club is funded in large part by a South African investment company, has former Springbok captain Francois Pienaar on the board and ex-SARFU chief executive Edward Griffiths in that role alongside Venter is a pretty strong case for viewing the North London outfit as a 'foreign' operation. However, the squad also contains some of the brightest English talent in the game, spearheaded by full back/No. 10 Alex Goode, flanker Andy Saull, wing Noah Cato and centre Adam Powell. The coaching team is headed by McCall along with Andy Farrell, Alex Sanderson and Paul Gustard, and while no one at Sarries envisaged this group would have to assume the lead role so quickly they handled the Leicester final with assurance.

It is Venter's fervent hope that when the time comes for him to return on a full-time basis to his GP practice in the Western Cape, the young English coaches in the current set-up – Farrell, Sanderson and Gustard – will be ready to step up and take over even more responsibility alongside the experienced McCall. Sarries have endured too many upheavals in recent years, and Griffiths, the CEO, is adamant that the club is going to be pushing for honours on a regular basis under Venter's direction.

It hasn't all been about Venter and his rows with the RFU. Sarries' season also provided an opportunity for players to show just how good they were to a wider rugby public. Saracens hooker Schalk Brits was voted the Rugby Players' Association Player of the Year in his first season in the Guinness Premiership, while Goode is pushing for a place in the England team at full back or outside half. Joubert was marvellous at No. 8 and along with Brits would get into any other international team; however, the Springboks do not want them at this point.

Brits said: 'The last 12 months since I arrived in the UK have been absolutely phenomenal on and off the pitch and now having this award to add to everything else is very special indeed. There's something special happening at Saracens and I am happy to be part of it.'

The South African influence has been a real positive at Sarries, and Venter can take credit for sticking to his beliefs and building something that he is confident will last. Young English talent like flanker Saull are fully embracing the system Venter has instigated. Saull is learning from stars like Brits every day in training and said, 'We are scoring the tries because Schalk is an incredible specimen but the rest of the guys are getting there in support and offering him the option to offload and make the most of his breaks.

'I have asked him lots of times why he chose hooker when he could play wing, centre, scrum half or anywhere in the back row and the answer is that like all front-row guys he has a screw loose and just loves that battle they get into.'

Just like Venter.

Exeter Rising
the Chiefs Step Up to the Top Flight
by STEVE BALE

'And the simple fact of having won the Championship when Bristol had the advantage of their parachute payment after relegation is its own recommendation of Exeter's worth'

Until the rise of Exeter Chiefs, there had been no brand-new entrants into the Guinness Premiership since Worcester in 2004, and there are many going back to English league rugby's earliest days who by their rise and fall will forever stand as a reminder of the perils of the top flight. Worcester themselves, now replaced by Exeter, show how even the best intentions can pave the road to hell – if by hell we mean the RFU Championship, which certainly became it for Bristol as the first relegated team not to go straight back up since they themselves stayed down in 2004.

Equally, to survive even one season in the Premiership, Exeter will have to triumph over all the routine pessimism – based on long past experience and prevailing everywhere bar of course Sandy Park – that what goes up tends to come straight back down. But just like Worcester before them, if ever a club are set up to succeed in the Premiership, here they are. And the simple fact of having won the Championship when Bristol had the advantage of their £1.75 million parachute payment after relegation in 2009 is its own recommendation of Exeter's worth.

'No one can tell me there is a harder competition to win in rugby than the Championship,' said Exeter's coach Rob Baxter. 'You start out immediately on the back foot, getting on for £2 million down on whoever has come down.

'Every single part of it favours the relegated Premiership side. If you come through that competition, which was made even harder last season, you have something special in your side, and you have to keep that culture.'

RIGHT Premiership here we come! Exeter celebrate, after their convincing Championship final second leg victory over Bristol, for a 38-16 aggregate win, gives them a place in English rugby's top tier.

Whether this means Exeter will be ready any time soon to challenge the primacy in the West Country of Bath and Gloucester is an open question which will have only a partial answer even if they have done well enough to avoid relegation when the dread moment arrives next May. But they did prove themselves over the season in the Championship, and more particularly in the convoluted play-off system which, having made it 'even harder', culminated in a narrow home win over Bristol followed by a thrashing of the same opposition at the Memorial Ground in the two-legged final.

If meticulous planning for a season-long campaign has anything to do with it, Baxter is perfectly qualified for the Premiership, having seen to it that his players put in the relevant mid-season training, which cost them a game or two but ensured they were at their strongest when it mattered most – against Bristol. This was a reminder of nothing so much as the way Wasps used to do it in those dominant years in mid-decade, when they never actually finished first in the Premiership but were always the best team in the league when it came to grand finals.

Exeter ended the regular season four points behind Bristol and it did not matter. 'We planned the season very, very well,' said Baxter. 'I was sick to the back teeth of people telling me we lost

those three games. This happened because we spent eight weeks in the gym already preparing for the climax.

'Being brave at the time paid off. We had said at the start that we had to win some games early on to gain momentum so that we didn't have to worry about being outside the top eight play-off places. That took a lot of pressure off.

'We then had to be prepared to lose a few games through the winter period. I was fortunate in my board of directors. I said they needed to back me when we lost some games over Christmas, because it was very likely that could happen.

'That's what kept us strong as a club. Everyone was talking about this losing streak, but did you see Exeter panicking about it? No, because we were in it together and we knew what we were doing.'

The question for now is about survival, but in the longer term it is whether Exeter have the wherewithal to provide a new focal point for rugby in a different part of the West from the Rec or Kingsholm. When you make the comparison in personnel, it will take some doing. Baxter himself did not expect to spend the full £4 million salary cap in the 2010-11 season, though a second season in the Premiership would be another matter. You would think he needed every penny he could get. There again, if Leeds could do it, so could Exeter.

If anyone personifies Exeter, it is Baxter, who had 14 years as a player including ten as first-team captain and was appointed coach before last season. Exeter have been Championship/National One runners-up three years in a row while all the time their ground alongside the M5 was being made fit for Premiership purpose. As it turned out last May, only the finalists had facilities that met Premiership criteria, Exeter having sold their old County Ground in the city for £11.4 million in 2004 and set about developing a stadium worthy of the elevated position they are now in as the 26th club to have played in the first tier. The trick now is to avoid going the way of Rosslyn Park, Rugby, Liverpool St Helens or more recently Rotherham. 'Moving to Sandy Park was the start of it, but look more closely at the last two or three seasons and we've steadily progressed,' said Baxter.

'Last season was the one we really backed ourselves. We had to fulfil Premiership criteria by the end of March and the Championship did not finish until late May. You take that gamble and say you are going for it.

'A few people said to me how fantastic and what a surprise it was that Exeter were in the Premiership. But for me it's not that fantastic or surprising, because we've worked towards developing a Premiership-level stadium over a number of years and we can develop further.

'We were very aware there would also be a lot of hard work in putting a team together who can be competitive the next season but was our performance at Bristol any less of a performance than Leeds were putting in at the same time in 2009?'

The answer to that is a resounding no, and as Worcester painfully discovered, Leeds were more than capable of holding their own in the Premiership after a slow start which turned out to misrepresent how competitive a Premiership side they would be. All of which having been said, Baxter remains a proponent of an enlarged Premiership – to 14 – which would have spared Worcester and accommodated Bristol as well as his Chiefs.

Maybe the financial constraints caused at the Memorial Ground by the second-season loss of Bristol's parachute payment make the thesis somewhat less tenable than it seemed at the end of last season, when the two legs of the final were played before packed houses, but Premiership expansion will eventually be on the agenda.

'Bristol are a big club and they've proved that by being in the Premiership as much as they have,' said Baxter. 'Nobody can tell me this is the way it should happen.

'You know and I know that, whichever way you try to dress it up, it's nonsense that what happened when Bristol played Exeter couldn't be happening in the Premiership week in week out for both ourselves and Bristol.

'The play-offs were the way it was decided it would run last season. I am not a big fan. I see how hard we've had to work and how much investment we've had to make to get a Premiership-ready club put together, so I know how Bristol had to work as well.

'Let us play Premiership rugby and, if the next Championship club come along and make that investment and get themselves ready, give them the opportunity. I'm not talking about getting rid of promotion and relegation.

'If the team who win the Championship have everything in place, they should come up and swap with whoever finishes bottom of the Premiership.'

Which is precisely what Exeter – who could be said to be the new Worcester in a number of ways – have already done, but by a considerably more circuitous route.

Down to the Final Play
the 2009-10 Guinness Premiership

by CHRIS HEWETT

'For much of a game rightly hailed as the best Grand Final to date, there was nothing between the contestants. The advantage swung this way and that'

Just when English club rugby needed a quiet season to reflect on the excesses and transgressions of the previous campaign – the fake blood affair at Harlequins, the drugs-related scandals at Bath, the coaching fallout that cost such gifted and resourceful operators as Richard Hill, Dean Ryan and the soon-to-be-knighted Ian McGeechan their jobs – along came Saracens. Or rather, the new Saracens, full of bristling intent and packed to the ceiling with South Africans. They would be unconventional, uncontrollable, unapologetic; indeed, some would come to regard them as unhinged. This much was certain: they were anything but quiet.

It was not until the long Guinness Premiership journey reached its halfway point – round 11 in late December – that they lost a league game, narrowly at London Irish. No one at Vicarage Road could have expected such a handsome return on their initial investment, although it was obvious from the opening two or three matches that some of the summer signings from Springbok country, the hooker Schalk Brits and the No. 8 Ernst Joubert in particular, constituted excellent pieces of business. Not that Saracens made too many friends. Their early-season rugby was more honoured in the breach than in the observance: it was cautious, conservative, narrowly focused and wholly dominated by the boot. As Richard Cockerill, the head coach at Leicester, was heard to say: 'You have to take them on in the scrum because it's the only time the ball is on the floor.'

The first meeting between the two sides was something of a game-changer for the entire competition. After the Tigers had scrummaged their way to an important victory in Watford, the Saracens director of rugby, Brendan Venter, treated the media to a 31-minute soliloquy on the subject of referees, the main thrust of which was that everyone was cheating except Saracens. 'I'm a positive person,' said the man from Cape Town. 'I normally have a plan for things and I'm good at following rules if I know what the rules are. I'm disciplined: discipline is one of the things on which I base my life and the things we do at this club. At the end of a game, I want to be able to shake someone's hand and say: "Fair enough, you whipped us." I can't say that today because I don't understand what went on out there. This is not how rugby is supposed to work.'

LEFT Leicester Tigers celebrate after their last-gasp 33-27 triumph over Saracens in the Premiership final at Twickenham.

Venter found himself deep in the disciplinary soup for this little outburst, and it would not be the last time. But he had lifted the lid on a problem surrounding the officiating at the tackle area, which placed ball carriers under serious threat of turnovers and convinced many teams that the only sensible option was to kick the skin off it, especially in their own half. The Rugby Football Union would never admit it publicly, but the South African's words set in train a process that would result in a refereeing adjustment that recalibrated the breakdown and, in the eyes of many observers, transformed the quality of the spectacle.

Pre-rant, only London Irish and Northampton had shown much in the way of adventure. Post-rant, everyone felt free to have a go with ball in hand. There were other factors, of course: better weather and firmer pitches helped the likes of Bath to reignite their counterattacking game and, by extension, rediscover the best of themselves. Wasps, hit hard by the departures of quality players during the summer, also felt able to move forward with confidence as the surfaces firmed up, and by the end of the season, there was a good deal to admire from Gloucester too. But it was the effect on Saracens that took the breath away. Their casting off of the shackles – by all accounts, a beer-fuelled bonding session down Brighton way resulted in a conscious change of approach (once they had regained consciousness, one assumes) – took opponents completely by surprise, and with brilliant home-grown youngsters like the full back Alex Goode and the flanker Andy Saull tripping the light fantastic, Venter's men turned around a mid-season slump and strung together a sensational run of results, spiced with ever more sensational tries.

Bath also made things happen in the second half of the campaign. The returns from injury of Butch James and Olly Barkley reinvigorated their midfield, and this jump-started Michael Claassens

RIGHT Leeds Carnegie stand-off Ceiron Thomas defies the rain to kick one of his four penalties as his side defeat Worcester Warriors 12-10 to stay in the Premiership.

FACING PAGE Joe Maddock leaves Ugo Monye and David Strettle flat out as he scores for Bath in their 24-13 home win over Harlequins in late March.

and Joe Maddock, both of whom had been out of sorts pre-Christmas. There was also a wholly positive contribution from Luke Watson, another of the season's high-calibre South African imports. His energy, leadership and finely honed offloading skills made him one of the stand-out loose forwards in the competition; indeed, at his best, he was every bit as influential as Joubert, his countryman, proved to be at Saracens.

The West Countrymen won 11 of their last dozen Premiership fixtures, having prevailed in only one of their first ten. But there were other teams in the shake-up, and one of them, the ever mighty Leicester, proved too strong for them. The swarming, suffocating sharp-end work of Louis Deacon, Jordan Crane, Marcos Ayerza and the exciting new tight-head prop Dan Cole made the Tigers horribly difficult to beat at Welford Road, even though Saracens managed it on the last afternoon of the regular season – a game that put Venter in more strife with the disciplinary classes, who ultimately decided to throw the book at him by banning him from Twickenham on Grand Final day. But more of that anon.

With London Irish falling away after a decent start – their injury count crippled them at important moments – and Wasps failing to convince up front despite a marked improvement in their scrummaging under the guidance of the World Cup-winning prop Trevor Woodman, the play-off places were relatively clear cut. Leicester and Saracens made it through with some comfort, as did Northampton, whose form stayed strong throughout. Only once did Jim Mallinder's side lose consecutive Premiership games, and that was not until April, when they were maxing out on their squad rotation. Come the final weekend, Bath alone needed victory to qualify for a semi-final slot, and as they were playing Leeds at home, the odds on them messing up were long indeed.

Not that Leeds were anyone's pushovers. One or two educated pundits always suspected they might have the wherewithal to stay up, given the amount of drive, expertise and honest-to-goodness realism associated with their coaches, Andy Key and Neil Back. So it proved. There were low moments: smashed at Headingley by London Irish in September, they turned in a ghastly 80 minutes against a struggling Gloucester side at the same venue a couple of weeks later. But they were working hard for each other, especially in the pack where it mattered, and with the likes of Mike MacDonald, Erik Lund, Hendre Fourie and the magnificent Marco Wentzel punching their weight to the very last ounce, their fortunes began to turn. A bloody-minded victory at Wasps was the initial galvaniser, and things fell into place with five wins in eight games between the end of February and the end of April.

Although Sale and Newcastle looked vulnerable at times, Worcester were the ones under threat. The Midlanders had useful performers in all roles except those they had struggled to fill since rising to the Premiership in 2004: scrum half and outside half, two of the crucial decision-making positions on the field. In the penultimate round, they found themselves travelling to Leeds knowing nothing short of victory would stave off relegation. They finished marginally short in a deeply neurotic encounter and ended on entirely the wrong note, two of their players – the flankers Chris Cracknell and James Collins – becoming embroiled in a tawdry terrace fracas also involving their own fathers.

So it was that Leicester, the hardy perennials and arch-traditionalists, met Saracens, the agitprop modernists, on a wet May day at Twickenham to settle the season's business once and for all. Venter, whose fiery exchanges with members of the Welford Road crowd in the last round of league matches had earned him a ten-week match-day coaching ban and left him persona non grata at Twickenham for the duration of the big event, watched proceedings at his home in St Albans. And what proceedings they turned out to be.

For much of a game rightly hailed as the best Grand Final to date, there was nothing between the contestants. The advantage swung this way and that – two very decent Leicester tries were more than matched by two absolute belters from Saracens, both finished by Joubert down the left – and even when

the Tigers tight forwards started imposing themselves at the set-piece in the third quarter, they could never quite find a way of shutting their opponents up.

With less than three minutes left on the clock, Venter's men went ahead through a Glen Jackson penalty. Job done? Not quite. Toby Flood, growing in authority and patently the form outside half in England, reached for his slide rule and dropped a millimetre-perfect restart over the head of Scott Hamilton, who claimed possession and sent Ben Youngs scampering towards the Saracens 22. Jackson caught him high, referee Dave Pearson appeared to signal a penalty, the rest of the defenders stopped – half in surprise, half in despair – and Dan Hipkiss, fresh off the bench, took full advantage of the hesitancy to bag the winning try.

A nine-month season, decided in the 81st minute of the last match. That's the modern club game for you: full of sound, fury … and wonderful finishes.

LEFT Northampton Saints stare down the barrel of semi-final elimination. Saracens hooker Schalk Brits has just levelled the scores with an injury-time try. Glen Jackson made no mistake with the conversion.

ABOVE At Twickenham, Saracens suffered in similarly dramatic fashion. Here Dan Hipkiss pounces to score the winning try late in the game.

PROTECTING WHAT YOU 🤍

Wishing Wooden Spoon every success

 INSURANCE 🤍 PENSIONS
INVESTMENTS

Saints Strike Silver the 2010 LV= Cup Final

by **PAUL BOLTON**

'Gloucester appeared to have regained the upper hand again when they were awarded a penalty try for a collapsed scrum, but Northampton's response was swift and effective'

Northampton ended their long search for a first major domestic title with a resilient performance in a pulsating first LV= Cup final that produced some breathtaking rugby at Worcester's Sixways Stadium. It gave Northampton's coaching team of Jim Mallinder and Dorian West their fourth trophy in three seasons in charge, following a National One and National Trophy double two years ago and the European Challenge Cup in 2009. Northampton's win also secured them a place in next season's Heineken Cup.

ABOVE Northampton Saints prop Soane Tonga'uiha touches down in the 32nd minute for his side's first try. The Tongan loose-head went on to be named man of the match at Sixways.

'There has been a lot of talk this season about the quality, or lack of quality, in the Premiership, but what an advert for the English game that was,' Mallinder said.

'For us, it is an important step to get some silverware and to show how much we have progressed as a club in recent seasons.

'But it was a very close game, and we had to defend superbly at times to keep Gloucester out.

'Overall, though, I am just happy we have won. It's all very well being involved in the shake-up in three competitions but if you end up not winning anything it's a fairly pointless boast.'

Gloucester's defeat was their fourth in a final since they won this competition seven years ago, but they could not be accused of choking in a big match on this occasion. The Kingsholm side contributed fully to the entertainment despite fielding a patched-up team missing a dozen front-line players, their spirit typified by England centre Mike Tindall, who flew back from Paris to act as water-bottle-and-kicking-tee-carrier for his clubmates.

There were two turning points against Gloucester midway through the second half. First when television match official Graham Hughes ruled that Nicky Robinson did not ground the ball over the line, then when prop Soane Tonga'uiha intercepted close to his own line and bullocked away on a 70-yard sprint. From a try-scoring position, Gloucester had to scramble back to deny Tonga'uiha, Shane Geraghty and Brian Mujati at the opposite end – one of several helter-skelter moments in a fast and furious contest. 'I thought, when I looked at the television replay on my monitor, that Robinson was just short when he claimed that try, and I also thought that Dowson's arm got underneath the ball,' Mallinder said.

Northampton centre James Downey scored the best try of the afternoon, sidestepping through after a series of glorious attacks and counterattacks while Gloucester lock Alex Brown was having treatment. The early departure of Brown and centre Tim Molenaar further depleted an already injury-ravaged Gloucester, but that did not stop the West Countrymen from testing Northampton to the limit.

The industrious Akapusi Qera crossed for a well-worked opener for Gloucester which was swiftly cancelled out by a close-range effort from Tonga'uiha. Gloucester appeared to have regained the upper hand again when they were awarded a penalty try for a collapsed scrum, but Northampton's response was swift and effective again, with scrum half Lee Dickson burrowing over.

Stephen Myler's accurate kicking embellished Northampton's 30-24 win in a final that would have graced Twickenham, from where it was moved because of the expected low turn-out on a Six Nations weekend. The semi-finals were played the previous week, which also gave the finalists little opportunity to sell tickets. Northampton, the only unbeaten side at the group stage, beat Saracens 31-20 in a grumpy contest at Franklin's Gardens.

Gloucester, meanwhile, ousted Cardiff Blues, the defending champions, at the Cardiff City Stadium, with James Simpson-Daniel scoring a hat-trick of tries in the 29-18 win. Simpson-Daniel also featured prominently in a stunning Gloucester fightback in their final pool match, which secured their place in the semi-finals. Gloucester were 20-0 down against Harlequins at the Twickenham Stoop, but then scored five tries, two of them from Simpson-Daniel, to snatch a 31-29 win.

The group stages of the inaugural LV= Cup included a novel playing format. The 16 sides were organized into four pools of four teams each. The teams from Pool 1 played those in Pool 4, and those in Pool 2 played those in Pool 3, each team therefore being guaranteed four pool matches. Confusing maybe, but coaches, players and spectators did not appear to mind. Though matches were played on international weekends, the competition produced some exhilarating rugby, none better than that played in a cracking final.

ABOVE Gloucester speedster James Simpson-Daniel is caught by Jon Clarke and Shane Geraghty. Simpson-Daniel had been prolific in earlier rounds, but there was no place for him on the scoresheet at Sixways.

FACING PAGE Scrum half Lee Dickson evades Rory Lawson to score Northampton's third try after 54 minutes.

FOLLOWING PAGES Northampton enjoy their LV= Cup success.

A Very Mixed Bag
the 2009-10 Heineken Cup

by **DAVID HANDS**

'On the other hand, Ngwenya did score one of the tries of the season, a magisterial 90-metre effort in which he stood up, among others, Wales wing Shane Williams'

European Rugby Cup Ltd (ERC), the organising body for the two European competitions, concluded they had something to celebrate in the 15th season of the Heineken Cup. Quite why, no one was very sure – we are not talking about silver or golden jubilees here – yet there were celebratory dinners and an eclectic team of the tournament, while on the field, where the true value lies, came a very mixed bag. A season which began under the long shadow cast by the 2008-09 'Bloodgate' scandal (the use by Harlequins of fake blood capsules during the Heineken Cup quarter-final against Leinster) seldom shook itself free of controversy. ERC were not short of critics of their disciplinary procedures as Bloodgate ran its course, and during 2009-10 they had also to deal with one of rugby's worst cases of gouging and the farcical elements of the '16th man' during the pool game between Ospreys and Leicester.

That the tournament ended with an all-French final was unsatisfactory too. Not, of course, for France, who enjoyed such an outstanding Six Nations and were delighted to see Toulouse and Biarritz compete for Europe's premier club honour at the Stade de France. But the essence of cross-border competition is that the best of one country should compete against the best of another, rather than reproduce a fixture which can be enjoyed in domestic tournaments.

How significant is it that the winners of the Guinness Premiership (Leicester), the Top 14 (Clermont Auvergne) and the Magners League (Ospreys) all failed to reach the semi-finals of the Heineken Cup? It is arguable that economic restrictions, certainly in England, mean there is insufficient squad depth for clubs to offer genuine competition on more than one front, even for so wealthy an organisation as Toulouse, who won the Heineken Cup for the fourth time (and had the T-shirts to prove it) but hardly in the grand manner.

And yet there remains a beauty to the tournament that has been true since its inaugural season. The Heineken Cup splashed colour through the first half of a season bogged down by negative play in both France and England; clubs threw off shackles and played wonderful rugby. In the first weekend of pool competition alone there was a shock defeat for the holders, Leinster, on their own turf; perennial favourites Munster crashed away to unconsidered Northampton; and there was utter drama in the drawn game at Welford Road between Leicester and Ospreys.

By the time the dust had settled and the quarter-finalists were known, France had four representatives still standing, Ireland two, England and Wales one each. There were gloomy predictions made in England until it was remembered that a year earlier France themselves had provided only one quarter-finalist, and that by the skin of their teeth. The impact of the Lions tour to South Africa in 2009 was certainly felt by the leading English and Welsh clubs, an impact softened for Leinster and Munster because of the frequency with which they rest players during the Celtic season.

Leinster were happy enough to reach the last eight after opening their defence by losing to London Irish on a rainy night at the RDS ground in Dublin. Two penalty goals by Peter Hewat and two more by Ryan Lamb gave the Exiles their 12-9 win, which proved something of a mirage since they achieved consistency in neither the Heineken Cup nor the Premiership, whereas Leinster, in Michael Cheika's last season as coach, put their show very firmly back on the road.

Less than 24 hours later, Munster were left reeling by the young Northampton lock Courtney Lawes, who gave a display of such maturity in his club's 31-27 win that even Paul O'Connell, the Lions captain, had to take second place. Shane Geraghty, too, twinkled his way through the Munster defence, though as it happened neither Lawes nor Geraghty had done enough to convince the England management of their sustained value.

Another day, another drama. Leicester, the beaten 2009 finalists, were dead in the water, 15 points down to the Ospreys and going nowhere, until a young centre called Billy Twelvetrees answered the call. Twelvetrees did not even know he was playing until ten minutes before the start, but by the finish he had scored a try, kicked three conversions and a penalty, and as near as damn it scored another try which would have won Leicester the game instead of leaving the scores tied at 32-32. For the rest of the season, Twelvetrees hardly featured either.

The next weekend, in the southwest corner of France, Biarritz served notice of intent when they recorded 42 points against Gloucester, the young United States wing Takudzwa Ngwenya scoring

FACING PAGE Imanol Harinordoquy, wearing a face guard to protect a broken nose, rises to claim the ball for Biarritz against Toulouse in the Heineken Cup final at Stade de France.

three tries with searing pace that Gloucester simply could not handle. As it turned out, they were not alone, but while Ngwenya was leaving others for dead, a trio of Englishmen – Magnus Lund, Iain Balshaw and Ayoola Erinle – were helping Biarritz along the road that led to Paris.

Rugby's darker side emerged in the second tranche of pool fixtures, in deep December. The clash of Ulster and Stade Français was marred when two accusations of gouging (both on the Ireland flanker Stephen Ferris) were made against Julien Dupuy and David Attoub, scrum half and prop respectively for the Parisian club. A disciplinary panel duly swung into action, amid claims by Stade Français that a photograph showing Attoub's offence and taken by a respected news agency representative had been doctored.

The upshot was a six-month ban for Dupuy (who had been Leicester's scrum half in the final the previous season), reduced by a week on appeal. It kept him out of the entire Six Nations, but Attoub's punishment was even longer: he was banned for 70 weeks for what Judge Jeff Blackett, the Rugby Football Union's disciplinary officer who heard the case, described as 'the worst act of contact with the eyes that I have had to deal with'.

The sentence also reflected the fact that many in the northern hemisphere considered various gouging offences that had taken place in the southern hemisphere during 2009 had been handled too leniently. Max Guazzini, the Stade Français president, was appalled: 'We tumbled upon an over-zealous judge and with an anti-French bias,' he said, and described Dupuy's punishment as 'political'.

But the tournament rolled on: Munster pulled off a magnificent 37-14 win at Perpignan, home of the French champions, and Leicester's display at home to Clermont Auvergne suggested new

stars were emerging for England in Dan Cole and Ben Youngs. In the final round of pool games, however, Leicester tumbled out in Swansea, and Northampton, securing a losing bonus point against Munster in Limerick in a game where they were strangely limited in their approach, went through into the last eight as England's only representative.

Leicester did not go quietly. In the final quarter of the Tigers' 17-12 loss to the Ospreys, the Welsh region

RIGHT Leicester's Billy Twelvetrees, who scored 14 points in the match, kicks upfield during the round one clash with Ospreys at Welford Road. The game ended 32-32.

ABOVE: 'Over the hills and far away ...' Takudzwa Ngwenya of Biarritz zips clear to score his third try of the home match against Gloucester.

FACING PAGE: Munster's Jean de Villiers tries to halt both Ben Foden and the impressive Shane Geraghty at Franklin's Gardens, where the Saints beat the Irish province 31-27.

played for nearly a minute with 16 men on the pitch after Lee Byrne returned from injury without the referee, Alan Lewis, knowing. The immediate aftermath reflected little credit on the game, Leicester complaining that their legitimate concerns were not addressed and that the subsequent enquiry should have been handled differently, while Lewis described what happened as an 'absolute nonsense'.

The Ospreys were fined 25,000 Euros and Byrne handed a two-week ban, though on appeal that was commuted to a 5000-Euro fine which allowed him to play for Wales against England on the opening day of the Six Nations. It did not get Leicester back into the tournament via a rematch, which some of their officials had hinted at, nor should it have done, and as the season neared its climax, France and Ireland dominated.

Northampton were despatched in the quarter-finals by Munster, and remarkably there were two 29-28 scorelines on successive days: the first favoured Leinster, on a day when Clermont Auvergne would surely have won had Brock James, their fly half, brought his kicking boots to Dublin. The second favoured Biarritz, who were doubly fortunate in that the Ospreys were denied a last-minute penalty attempt which would have won them the game.

On the other hand, Ngwenya did score one of the tries of the season, a magisterial 90-metre effort in which he stood up, among others, Wales wing Shane Williams. It carried Biarritz to a semi-final with Munster in which Imanol Harinordoquy, the outstanding France No. 8, played with a facial guard (to protect a broken nose) and had to be dragged off with damaged ribs after ensuring his club would reach the final.

There were hints, along the way, that Munster have lost some of their European magic, though such has been their quality over an 11-year period that few will rush to write them off. Meanwhile Toulouse, having disposed of Stade Français in the quarter-finals, now did the same with Leinster, their scrum reducing the Irish province to a game of fits and starts while David Skrela kicked his goals and scored a try for a match haul of 21 points.

Toulouse went into their sixth Heineken final as favourites, and even when Biarritz took a 9-3 lead thanks to the kicking of Dimitri Yachvili, there was a sense that their advantage was illusory. So it proved: Toulouse used their scrum as the ultimate weapon and squeezed their opponents out, Skrela and Florian Fritz peppering the posts with penalties and dropped goals to take a 21-12 lead. Yet with seven minutes remaining, Ngwenya – badly underused by Biarritz on the day – scorched clear and sent Karmichael Hunt over for a try which, converted by Valentin Courrent, left only two points between the teams. Could Biarritz provide the fairy-tale ending? They could not: their opponents' pack resumed their iron grip and the trophy was Toulouse's again.

PRIORITY

Our customers can get Priority treatment
at Twickenham on match days

Visit o2.co.uk/rugby for more details

ENGLAND
RUGBY

We're better, connected

O2

Blue Heaven
the 2010 Challenge Cup Final

by TERRY COOPER

'They turned a ray of hope no bigger than a match-flame into a raging, game-winning burst that contained tries for centre Jamie Roberts, wing Leigh Halfpenny and lock Bradley Davies'

It's time we ceased calling the Challenge Cup 'the second-tier European tournament' or 'the junior competition'. The event has grown massively in stature, and its reputation was further enhanced by a superb afternoon of rugby on the shores of the Mediterranean. Not for the first time in recent seasons a magnificent Challenge final, won so admirably by Cardiff Blues in the marvellous Marseille Vélodrome, comfortably outclassed the Heineken final in terms of spectacle, fluctuation and tension.

European Rugby Cup's bold and imaginative decision – a phrase seldom used – to take a final to a Test match venue was vindicated, and Blues had no problems that the ground is a short drive from

ABOVE Second-row Bradley Davies dives in to score Cardiff Blues' third try at Marseille.

Toulon. The Twickenham Stoop, Madejski Stadium and Kingsholm have served recent Challenge finals well enough, but in future bigger-capacity stadia must be used. Yes, that makes it difficult to hold a final in England unless ERC take the Twickenham Stadium option. Blues were also ultimately very content with another ERC initiative that allowed the three best non-qualifiers in the Heineken to drop down to the Challenge Cup quarter-finals, the others being Scarlets and Gloucester.

The result in Marseille certainly hinged on a few seconds of play soon after half-time, when Toulon led 13-6 and were awarded a penalty that was a six-inch putt for Jonny Wilkinson. Juan Martín Fernández Lobbe chose to run the ball, and when the move went wrong Wilkinson bailed out of a drop-kick attempt and fell over in a heap. He recovered and was instantly able to try a penalty at goal. Again he collapsed as the ball missed, and there was the routine sight of Jonny being helped off. He thought it might be 'a back spasm or broken rib' but was able to depart with England to Australia a few days later. The tactic was a monumental blunder by Fernández Lobbe, who had dozily mistimed a glaring scoring pass in the opening spell. The let-off changed Cardiff's mood. They turned a ray of hope no bigger than a match-flame into a raging, game-winning burst that contained tries for centre Jamie Roberts, wing Leigh Halfpenny and lock Bradley Davies in a mere 18 minutes. It brought a European trophy to Wales for the first time in 15 seasons of competition that began when Cardiff as a club lost to (of course) Toulouse in the first Heineken final.

In typical French fashion, Toulon owner Mourad Boudjellal was stunningly frank about Fernández Lobbe's moment of rugby insanity. 'We had the game, then we lost it. It was unacceptable not to kick at goal when we led by only seven. I'm angry with the players. They only had to give it to Jonny. We lost because we did not respect the Blues.' His bitterness must have been intensified by Toulon's double whammy, because his expensively assembled outfit had lost in the semi-finals of the Top 14 play-offs one week earlier.

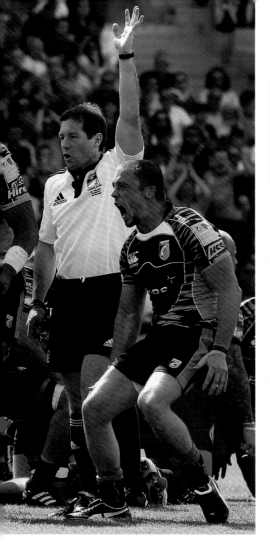

LEFT Cardiff's Wales and Lions centre Jamie Roberts celebrates opening his side's try account.

FOLLOWING PAGES Cardiff Blues – the first Welsh side to lift a European club/regional rugby title.

Toulon coach Philippe Saint-André took a wider view. 'We broke their defence seven or eight times and should have led by 20 points. Maybe if we had taken the penalty … We would have led by ten and Jonny would not have been hurt.'

Blues coach Dai Young had no doubts that the removal of their tormentor opened the way. 'It was the key. When we were putting pressure on, Jonny was able to relieve that. We were playing into his hands and hanging on by our toenails, though we are a second-half side and were confident that we would come strongly.'

Toulon gave early notice of their wasteful ways when they chucked away a chance within seconds of the kick-off. Leigh Halfpenny's long penalty was matched by Wilkinson, who levelled again after Ben Blair had made it 6-3. Blues' brief leads were mere punctuations in a half featuring sweeping attacks down the touch lines by the French that induced frenzy then frustration in their supporters, who comprised about 99 per cent of the 49,000 audience.

Overambition and careless passing plus a jaw-dropping display of relentless tackling kept Blues' goal line intact until the 36th minute when Sonny Bill Williams – a dominant force when Toulon were in control – carved past three men following a move that explored both sides of the pitch. Wilkinson converted and in the second half the contest continued for a few minutes down its one-way *rue*.

During the Wilkinson–Fernández Lobbe fiasco there were hints of disagreement, and when it went pear-shaped … Well, we all know what happens when French rugby teams start arguing among themselves. Meltdown. Tom May immediately fumbled a ball behind his own line and Blues pounced. Their scrum, which had struggled in the opening half, pulled themselves together and forced a free kick. Xavier Rush and Martyn Williams came close and Richie Rees cleverly gave Roberts the scoring pass. Roberts admitted later: 'I didn't touch the ball in the first half,' and the rise in his influence was another indication that the balance had swung drastically.

Blair converted for 13-13, then he and May swapped penalties for another hung-parliament situation. The cup was won when centre Casey Laulala's strength and vision twice opened Toulon's defence inside the final quarter. He made tries for Halfpenny and Davies, the latter coming from another scrum free kick, and Cardiff could absorb a late try from Thomas Sourice to finish winners by 28 points to 21. Cardiff's success created a place by the back door for Scarlets in the 2010–11 Heineken. Gloucester, hoping for a Toulon win to gain Heineken entry by the tradesmen's entrance, were denied.

In his euphoria Coach Young gave the region optimism about next season's Heineken. 'I am not going to make bold, specific statements that we can win it, but there is no reason why we cannot go all the way, we will be in the hunt and nobody will underestimate us.'

No team will host Cardiff without a tremor, after their Euro campaign included stirring away wins, notably at Wasps and at this supposed neutral venue. They reached the final by beating Newcastle 55-20 in the quarter-finals and Wasps 18-15 in the semis. Toulon knocked out Scarlets 38-12 and beat Connacht in Galway 19-12 at the same stages.

REVIEW OF THE
SEASON 2009-10

France's Full House
the 2010 Six Nations Championship
by CHRIS JONES

'France signalled their credentials as potential Slam winners with a 33-10 victory over reigning champions Ireland in Paris, scoring three tries'

One match and one sickening incident had a profound effect on the 2010 RBS Six Nations Championship, which concluded in a rainswept Paris with France securing the Grand Slam with their least expansive performance of the campaign to defeat an improving England side 12-10. It was France's first Slam since 2004 and their ninth overall (including six in the Five Nations), and watching on television was Thom Evans, the Scotland wing, whose neck was so seriously injured in the match against Wales in Cardiff – in a collision with Wales full back Lee Byrne – that the flying wing was forced to quit rugby on medical advice.

To lose a player of such obvious talent at just 25 years old is a sobering reminder to everyone in rugby about the injuries that can happen in a collision sport that is getting more explosive every year. This one was caused by a freak accident as Evans' head hit Byrne in the midriff as they came together. All the Scotland players, including Thom's brother Max, could only watch from a distance as the medical staff, led by Scotland's Dr James Robson, tended to the stricken player on the Millennium Stadium turf.

Evans credits Robson with saving his life, and this is just the latest example of his medical expertise being shown in the most chaotic of circumstances. Robson was able to identify the potentially catastrophic problem and use his skills to keep Evans in a position that did not further damage his neck. Evans cannot play rugby again, but intends to use his sporting prowess on the golf course and can look forward to new challenges, thanks to the help of all of the medical staff who treated him in Cardiff and, of course, the brilliance of Robson.

The injury apart, the day had gone well for Scotland as they produced the kind of high-intensity and physical rugby that head coach Andy Robinson preaches, to such an extent that Wales fell off tackles and found themselves trailing 24-14 with four minutes to go. Instead of capitulating, Wales staged a remarkable comeback that would give this game legendary status, and it was fitting that their greatest try scorer of all time – Shane Williams – should dive over the line (arm raised in triumph before he even reached the whitewash) to send an entire nation delirious and leave Scotland stunned 31-24.

It was all too much for Andy Powell, the Wales back-row forward, who just hours after helping Wales complete that stunning comeback victory was arrested for, and admitted to, driving a golf buggy on the M4 while drunk. It was a stupid prank that saw the player dumped from the squad and raised yet more questions about the Welsh players and their ability to handle themselves in the glare of publicity. With Gavin Henson opting out of rugby due to repeated injury problems, this was a season of great highs and debilitating lows for the Welsh.

Wales would finish fourth, with Ireland, 2009 Grand Slam winners, coming second with three victories and two defeats and boasting, in wing Tommy Bowe, the Player of the Championship.

ABOVE Shane Williams begins his celebrations before touching down for the winning try for Wales against Scotland at the Millennium Stadium.

FACING PAGE France's Mathieu Bastareaud is congratulated by his colleagues after scoring against Scotland at Murrayfield.

Despite defeating England and Wales, Ireland failed to win the Triple Crown after a 23-20 defeat to the always competitive Scots in their final match. England were third, and like Wales recorded two wins in the championship, while Scotland and Italy finished in fifth and sixth positions for the third tournament in a row. Both managed just one win, although Scotland also recorded a draw in the Calcutta Cup match against England to ensure they ended up one place ahead of Italy in the table.

Ireland's 27-12 victory over Wales on 13 March had seen Brian O'Driscoll record 100 caps for his country, something John Hayes had achieved in the previous match with England. Hayes thus became the first Irish player to join the centurions of rugby – a remarkable feat given he is a front-row forward who has often been described as the team's weak link up front. How Hayes has proved the doubters wrong.

It was significant that four French players had contested the Player of the Championship poll with Bowe. Mathieu Bastareaud, who had proved that he could mentally recover from off-the-field problems on a recent tour to New Zealand; scrum half Morgan Parra; captain and flanker Thierry Dusautoir; and the amazing Imanol Harinordoquy – this was the quartet to be given extra recognition. Wales's mercurial Shane Williams was also in the hunt for the award, but it went to Bowe, who polled nearly 50 per cent of the fan votes.

It was two tries for Bastareaud that helped France start their campaign with a hard-fought 18-9 win against Scotland, who could only manage three Chris Paterson penalties on a weekend that also

saw Ireland begin their farewell season at Croke Park (Lansdowne Road is now ready for their return) with a 29-11 win over Italy. England, meanwhile, wore period-style kit to celebrate a centenary of matches with Wales and claimed a 30-17 win thanks to tries from James Haskell (two) and Danny Care plus Jonny Wilkinson's boot. Alun-Wyn Jones's sin-binning for a stupid trip was a key turning point.

The next round of matches was dominated by that Wales–Scotland encounter in Cardiff. Chris Paterson won his 100th cap, but Scotland used four different full backs during the game and finished with just four backs on the field, and crucially only 13 men, with replacements Scott Lawson and Phil Godman both in the sin-bin. There were just 12 seconds of normal time remaining when Godman (with head heavily bandaged) got his marching orders for tripping Lee Byrne after he chipped ahead and Stephen Jones kicked the penalty to tie the scores. There was now one play left and replacement scrum half Mike Blair – playing on the wing – had to take the kick-off. Wales claimed the ball and surged upfield to give Williams the chance to dart over under the posts for the win.

France signalled their credentials as potential Slam winners with a 33-10 victory over reigning champions Ireland in Paris, scoring three tries, plus 15 points from the boot of the increasingly influential Parra at scrum half. David Wallace grabbed a try for Ireland, with Ronan O'Gara kicking the other points in match that brought Ireland right down to earth with a bump.

England under Martin Johnson headed to Italy where they knew the locals would make it tough, and thanks to their own ineptitude the English only managed a tame 17-12 win. Captain Steve Borthwick tried to spin a line that England were getting better and had been, at times, outstanding in attack, but no one bought that one on an unhappy Valentine's Day in Rome. Jonny Wilkinson had an on-off day with the boot, missing two penalties as well as the conversion of Mathew Tait's try. It was also becoming clear that Wilkinson was not the answer to England's attacking play at No. 10.

Another brilliant Shane Williams try was not enough to help the Welsh pull off another remarkable win – this time at home to France, who had led 20-0 at half-time thanks to Welsh generosity. Leigh Halfpenny also got on the try-scoring list for Wales that Friday night, but tries by François Trinh-Duc and Alexis Palisson along with three Parra penalties and one from Freddy Michalak saw France home 26-20, despite being down to 14 men for half of the last quarter with Parra in the sin-bin.

Scotland had been warned about taking on Italy – a team who had beaten them before in Rome – and it turned out to be another banana skin thanks to a great break by Gonzalo Canale, who set up the winning try for Pablo Canavosio. Johnnie Beattie, part of the brilliant 'Killer Bees' Scots back row, had almost scored for the visitors, who lacked precision and had to once again rely on the boot to get their points. England, with Wilkinson still at No. 10, appeared ready to take Ireland at Twickenham, a Dan Cole try and a trademark Wikinson dropped goal putting them in control, only for their defence to fall apart off a line-out move. Tommy Bowe slipped past two tacklers to score and claim a 20-16 win that heaped more pressure on Johnson and his underperforming coaching staff.

Two tries from Keith Earls were crucial in the next round for the Irish, who looked a more potent force with Jonathan Sexton at No. 10 as they accounted for Wales 27-12 at Croke Park. The visitors were only able to manage four Stephen Jones penalties, setting Ireland up for that Triple Crown bid against the Scots on the final weekend of the championship. England's poor play continued to anger their fans, although the 15-15 draw against Scotland at Murrayfield featured an explosion of rage – caught on camera – from Andy Robinson. He knew the Scots had missed a golden opportunity to expose the limitations of the team he used to coach. Wilkinson went off with a head injury early in the second half, to be replaced by Toby Flood, who was later to start at fly half against the French, with Wilkinson named on the bench.

Marc Lièvremont, who had taken so much stick by constantly chopping and changing his team in the build-up to the 2010 season, was proving that his strategy as head coach had been correct as France remained unbeaten with a thumping 46-20 win over Italy in Paris. David Marty scored two of the team's six tries as the Italians were constantly torn apart in midfield by the fast-moving French, who it appeared would have no trouble accounting for the England on the final weekend.

Wales found themselves dragged into a Wooden Spoon shoot-out against Italy and grabbed the headlines by handing wing Tom Prydie a debut, making him the youngest Test cap in Wales's history, at 18 years and 25 days. More significantly, Mike Phillips, the Lions scrum half, was fit. In the event his influence was key, while James Hook confirmed his standing as a game-breaker with two tries in a 33-10 win in which Shane Williams, inevitably, also got on the scoresheet. The victory took some of the heat off Warren Gatland, the head coach. Croke Park, meanwhile, did not have a Triple Crown to celebrate the departure of Ireland's rugby players, the Scots claiming a deserved 23-20 win thanks to Beattie's try and 18 points from the boot of Dan Parks.

All eyes were now on Paris, and while France claimed the Grand Slam, it was the English players who came of age under the captaincy of Lewis Moody, with the rest of the side following his example of never taking a backward step. Johnson finally gave Chris Ashton a chance on the wing, and while he ruined a great try-scoring chance, his partnership with Ben Foden proved England could play rugby and not just kick. There were no tries from France, but that didn't stop them celebrating with huge exuberance at the end of an excellent campaign.

ABOVE Dan Parks scored 18 of Scotland's 23 points in their victory over Ireland at Croke Park, including a last-minute penalty to steal the win.

FACING PAGE Replacement scrum half Pablo Canavosio strikes as Italy defeat Scotland 16-12 at Rome's Stadio Flaminio. Nevertheless, the Italians still ended up with the Wooden Spoon, going down to Wales in Cardiff on the last day of the Championship in the bottom-place decider.

The Club Scene
England: Year of New Trophies
by BILL MITCHELL

'The 2009-10 season saw the introduction of league champions cups, with finals at Twickenham, as a way of coming up with a single champion club at each level'

As usual one must start any summary of a country's achievements at all levels with an assessment of results in international encounters, and in the case of England it can be said 'could do better; sometimes unlucky; promising for the future'. Since the best estimate could also be applied to Scotland and others it should be emphasized that there is plenty of rivalry.

The internationals effectively have two seasons – autumn and spring – with the Six Nations Championship, and its possibility of a Grand Slam and/or Triple Crown, at stake in the latter, and England broke even over the piece, just about, with a summer moral bonus. In the autumn, three matches were played, with a victory over Argentina (16-9) being offset somewhat by defeats against Australia (9-18) and New Zealand (6-19). To be expected? Perhaps.

The Six Nations started well against careless Wales at Twickenham (30-17). This win was followed by an unconvincing but successful visit to the Stadio Flaminio in Rome (17-12), which brought defending champions Ireland to Twickenham (16-20), when a late missed tackle by the normally totally reliable Wilkinson was decisive. Visits to Murrayfield are often unsuccessful, and a draw (15-15) was probably the most reasonable result. England thus retained the Calcutta Cup, but both sides could feel aggrieved at a poor performance from South African referee Marius Jonker, who gave the impression that touch judges were there on suffrance and were to be ignored. Jonker also failed to deal with a fight after a Wilkinson penalty (well taken but should have been reversed). Meanwhile Scotland were denied by fortune when two Dan Parks penalties hit woodwork and rebounded.

But if England were lucky to emerge with a share of the points in Edinburgh, they were extremely unfortunate in Paris (10-12), with another southern hemisphere referee being openly hostile to the scrummaging to the extent that chief coach Martin Johnson openly remonstrated with him after a match that brought an undeserved Grand Slam to the Tricolores. This left a summer tour Down Under, and luck was only on their side in the second match in Australia (21-20) after an unlucky loss in the opener (17-27), the tour ending in a loss (28-35) to New Zealand Maori.

For their part, England Saxons generally had a good season and won the Churchill Cup in North America, beating Canada in the final (38-18). So things looked reasonably satisfactory, especially as

FACING PAGE Hard-tackling Cambridge centre Freddie Shepherd is brought down by the Oxford defence during the Varsity Match at Twickenham.

BELOW Emily Scarratt wrong-foots the France defence during the 11-10 victory that brought England Women a Six Nations Grand Slam in 2010.

ABOVE Gareth Steenson drops for goal as Exeter Chiefs beat Bristol 29-10 in the second leg of the Championship final. The fly half kicked 24 of Exeter's points.

FACING PAGE The Armitage brothers – Delon, Steffon and Guy – with the Russell-Cargill Memorial Trophy after London Irish's Middlesex Sevens triumph in August 2009.

England's age-group teams (Under 20 etc.) did well and the women won their Six Nations.

At times it seemed that Martin Johnson's job was at risk, so he will be hoping for a better new season supported by an excellent stock of young talent, even though much depends on whether the brilliant Danny Cipriani does not go to Australia. The pack is good and can only get better. Fans will hope that the vastly revised squad will do themselves justice, but it will require luck and hard work.

In the domestic game, the Guinness Premiership final at Twickenham was a thriller and brought success for Leicester over Saracens (33-27), thanks to a late injury-time try. In the inaugural Championship, Bristol beat London Welsh (28-15) and Exeter defeated Bedford (37-8) in the promotion play-off semi-finals, the Chiefs going on to beat Bristol over two legs in the final (38-16 on aggregate) to gain elevation to the top tier. In the final of the Anglo-Welsh competition, now the LV= Cup, Northampton gained a 30-24 victory over Gloucester at Sixways, while Cornish Pirates won the first final of the British & Irish Cup, beating Munster 23-14 at Camborne.

A little lower in the RFU league hierarchy, the 2009-10 season saw the introduction of league champions cups, with finals at Twickenham, as a way of coming up with a single champion club at each level. In the RFU structure, the Premiership equates to Level 1, the Championship to Level 2, National 1 to Level 3 and so on. The league champions cups were brought in at National 2 (Level 4), National 3 (Level 5) and Divisional 1 (Level 6) grades, where multiple divisions mean that there is no outright league champion without some sort of play-off competition. Macclesfield, Jersey and Hartpury College respectively were the inaugural winners of the league champions cups. Meanwhile, the RFU Intermediate Cup (for Level 7 clubs), Senior Vase (Level 8) and Junior Vase (Level 9 and lower) finals also took place at Headquarters, with Old Redcliffians, Brighton and Teddington triumphing this year.

Elsewhere, London Irish won the 2009 Middlesex Sevens, beating ULR Samurai Internationals in the final (26-19), while in December there was once again an excellent Varsity Match, with Cambridge winning (31-27), thanks largely to the superb tackling of centres Freddie Shepherd and Fred Burdon when the Dark Blues looked possible winners. The occasion was marred by the harsh dismissal early on in the Under 21 match of Cambridge captain Tom Stanton, which led to a massive 53-17 defeat for his side.

In the Babcock Inter-Services Championship, the Royal Navy emerged victorious, winning against both the RAF (73-3) and the Army (24-22). Meanwhile, the Barbarians soldier on despite the fact that they are not appreciated as they should be. An up-and-down season brought victories against a slightly understrength All Blacks outfit (25-18) and Ireland (29-23), while the Baa Baas went down against the Combined Services (19-22), England (26-35) and Bedford (14-50) in the Mobbs Memorial Match.

Last Words!
People reading this will note low marks for some referees with almost one common denominator – lower hemisphere origins. With some of the technology available and the scope for teamwork with colleagues, they should be better. The Calcutta Cup match was the nadir, and a poor showing by the official in Paris added to the embarrassment.

Scotland's victory in Dublin was achieved in spite of South Africa's Jonathan Kaplan failing to use available technology to disallow two home tries, while the Scots were possibly unlucky when Italy were awarded the try in Rome when obstruction seemed to have been evident.

The verdict? With the best will in the world, it must be said that the northern hemisphere has better officials, but will it make any difference to future appointments? Do not hold your breath. Neutrality does not bring greater efficiency.

Scotland: Third Top-Tier Club Needed?

by ALAN LORIMER

'Arguably Scotland get by with just two professional teams, but what is palpably missing is the competition for places that a larger pool of players would generate'

Just how much longer Scottish rugby can survive at international level with only two home-based professional clubs remains a constant talking point north of the border. And little wonder. For there is little doubt that the cull of the Borders pro team three years ago has shrunk the pool of players available to the national coach and that, in turn, is impacting on Scotland's international standing. Of the squad that took part in the 2010 Six Nations Championship, approximately one-third owe their international careers to initial contracts with the Borders, providing proof – if, indeed, it were needed – that a third professional club could make a significant contribution to the national team. Arguably Scotland get by with just two professional teams, but what is palpably missing is the competition for places that a larger pool of players would generate.

With the SRU coffers mirroring those of the UK government, the chances of Murrayfield resurrecting a third side, whether based in the Borders or elsewhere, look close to zero. Ownership (and hence control) of Scotland's professional teams remains with the SRU and, with debt reduction driving policy at Murrayfield, the rugby community north of the border, it seems, will have to accept that Edinburgh and Glasgow are not about to acquire a sibling club.

It was argued at the time of the cull that concentrating resources in two teams rather than spreading a diminishing pot across three clubs would strengthen the hand of the two survivors. Well, has it? To a degree there is mileage in this argument as this season has shown. But only to a degree. Without the kind of funding available to higher-spending clubs in the Magners League and more so in the Heineken Cup, Edinburgh and Glasgow remain as the poor relations of these two competitions, unable to afford star names to boost their performance levels and as a result competitively disadvantaged. Yet there is cause for optimism, particularly at Glasgow where the perennially underperforming side last season woke up to the idea that they could adopt a winning mentality.

Glasgow's collective form emerged from the arrival at the club of Chris Cusiter, the new-found confidence of Dan Parks and the gelling together of the three Bs – Johnnie Beattie, John Barclay and Kelly Brown – who went on to become a fixture in the Scotland back row. Add to that the zest of the Evans brothers – until the younger, Thom, suffered that dreadful injury against Wales – a big improvement in Graeme Morrison's game and the inspiring presence of lock Alastair Kellock and full back Bernardo Stortoni, and what transpired was a team that turned potential into a winning reality.

The prize was a place in the first ever Magners League play-offs after a third-place finish. In the event Glasgow lost to the eventual winners, Ospreys, in the semi-final round, but the point had been made. Glasgow woke up and a new era may have begun. But it will be an era without their key player, Dan Parks, who is now with Cardiff Blues, and their skilful flanker Kelly Brown, a Saracens signing this season.

Glasgow gave an indication of their ambition by running the eventual beaten finalists, Biarritz, close in the opening round of the Heineken Cup at Firhill, only to lose 18-22. But it was a false dawn for Glasgow, who could register only two wins – against Gloucester and the Dragons – to finish third in their pool. This season, with fly half Duncan Weir, centre Alex Dunbar and flanker Chris Fusaro among the new recruits, Glasgow should now have the confidence to build on last season's success.

Fifty miles to the east, Edinburgh, under new head coach Rob Moffat, who took over from Andy Robinson, slipped behind Glasgow after losing to the west club in back-to-back matches over the festive season and then suffering a slump in their final four matches, with a defeat to Connacht beginning the decline.

Edinburgh's fall from supremacy in Scotland undoubtedly had much to do with a loss of form among several key players allied to lengthy sidelining injuries suffered by Scotland caps Simon Webster, Ally Hogg and Ross Rennie. Rather alarmingly, Scotland skipper Mike Blair was not at his sharpest, but if this affected the team it allowed Greig Laidlaw, the nephew of the great Roy Laidlaw, to seize his chance and add to his growing reputation, enhanced by Sevens performances that helped Scotland to an impressive showing at the Edinburgh tournament in May.

LEFT Glasgow lock Richie Gray on the rampage against Edinburgh at Murrayfield. The Warriors did a Magners double over the capital side in 2009-10.

But in spite of their lower-than-expected finishing place in the Magners League, Edinburgh provided some thrilling spectacles for their Murrayfield fans, not least home wins over Cardiff, Munster, Ospreys and Scarlets. Edinburgh were riding high at the end of March, but then came the late-season slump, with four successive defeats wiping out all hopes of reaching the play-offs.

The Scottish capital side have lost their international forwards Jim Hamilton, Ally Hogg and Dave Callum along with back-row Simon Cross, but among an interesting crop of incomers to a squad increased from 36 to 40 are Alex Blair, the younger brother of Mike Blair; former Worcester centre Alex Grove; two exciting Borderers, James King and Lee Jones; and Scotland Under 20 forwards Stuart McInally and David Denton. That should give Moffat, whose desire to produce a fast, running game has made him popular with the home fans, a squad that can compete but that needs to find just a notch more of the killer instinct to achieve.

The meagre stock of professional players in Scotland has spawned talk of making the top end of the amateur leagues – the Premiership – a semi-pro competition based on a league of eight. There is little doubt that such a change is needed to provide a route for talented youngsters to progress and to create a vehicle capable of fulfilling the ambitions of more established players not considered for professional contracts.

BELOW Gordon Reid goes over to score late in the first half as Ayr outgun Melrose 36-23 to win the Scottish Hydro Premier Cup final at Murrayfield.

FACING PAGE Currie's John Cox runs at West of Scotland fly half Conor Davis at Burnbrae. Currie won this encounter 63-12 on their way to the Premiership first division title.

Unquestionably Scotland's top two 'amateur' clubs, Currie and Ayr, have edged in that direction. Their dominance during the 2009-10 season raised the bar in the Scottish Hydro league, asking questions of many of the more established clubs. In the end none could stay with the pace set by this duo and it became a straight battle between them, resulting finally in the league title going to Currie. But Ayr shared the season's honours after lifting the Scottish Hydro Cup with victory over Melrose in the final at Murrayfield.

Currie, coached by the former Scotland A fly half Ally Donaldson, reaped the rewards of ambition. Their achievement required several

careful signings in former New Zealand Under 21 lock Ryan Wilson and Kiwi full back Johnnie Smith, but crucially a vibrant youth section has produced a number of young players who stepped up to play their part in Currie's success, among them the Scotland Under 20 fly half Matthew Scott. Currie's investment in age-grade rugby brought its own success with victory for the club's Under 18 side over Dumfries in the final of the National Youth Cup at Murrayfield.

Melrose and Dundee, who both played some exceptionally attractive rugby over the season, filled the third and fourth spots in the league, while at the other end Edinburgh Accies and their near city neighbours Stewart's Melville went through the trap door, exchanging places with the Premier Two champions Stirling County and second-placed Hawick, the latter making a return to the top tier after a first ever season out of the first division.

If there was the perception that the top club sides were narrowing the gap between them and the professional teams, then a reality check was at hand in the shape of the British & Irish Cup competition. Scotland had three entrants – Gael Force, Heriot's and Ayr. In the event Gael Force, made up of young National Academy players, were blown away, losing their opening two matches to Cornish Pirates and Exeter Chiefs. Heriot's competed well, losing their opening match by 5-0 to Nottingham and playing good rugby in their remaining four matches but to no avail in terms of victory.

It was left to Ayr to carry the Scottish flag and they did so with some success, beating Rotherham Titans and Birmingham/Solihull and losing 21-22 to Pontypridd, 7-32 to Doncaster Knights and 27-30 to Cardiff to finish fourth. Ayr now know what they have to do to compete against professionals, and if their recent success in domestic competition is a guide to their ambition, they will achieve their goal.

And with Currie intent on a similar path and the likes of Melrose, Glasgow Hawks, Heriot's and Dundee ready to follow, Scottish club rugby looks set to enter a new era, a period perhaps when ambitious sides, eager to be free of the stultifying shackles of historical amateurism, can drive the game forward in Scotland, and maybe establish an alternative professional model to that of Murrayfield's central control. Scottish club rugby now needs a radical change. Perhaps now is the time to deliver.

Wales: Season of Silverware

by DAVID STEWART

'A post Lions tour season is always a heck of a challenge for players who have put their all into those wonderful adventures, and 2009-10 was no different'

Increasingly success is being measured by trophies won. On that basis, it was a good year. The Ospreys had the satisfaction of winning the inaugural Magners play-off, styled as a Grand Final. The Blues emerged from the latest campaign with further silverware in the form of the Amlin Challenge Cup. The Dragons will feel they too have made significant progress, but the outlook for the Scarlets is uncertain.

A glance at the Ospreys line-up shows so-called marquee names like Mike Phillips and Jerry Collins which reportedly attract salaries to match, so inevitably expectations are higher than with some of the neighbouring regions. Prior to Saturday 29 May (my word, what a long season it is now; pre-season friendlies start in mid-August) at the RDS in Dublin, their season was looking somewhat disappointing. A solid qualification from their Heineken group led to a quarter-final against Biarritz in lovely San Sebastián, where in summer heat they lost by a point 28-29. That represented a failure in the team's own eyes, given that the main European competition is the supreme goal nowadays.

A post Lions tour season is always a heck of a challenge for players who have put their all into those wonderful adventures, and 2009-10 was no different for Welsh and Irish players in particular as they made up the bulk of the Test team. Ospreys in that category included ever-presents Phillips and Tommy Bowe; other starters were Lee Byrne, Shane Williams, Adam Jones and Alun-Wyn Jones. Perhaps that was why once again this term there was a feeling that the squad had not met their considerable potential. Scott Johnson, alarmingly unwell at the time of the Biarritz game, had time to impose his influence upon the unit, which included a style of play which was nobly bold and attractive. So the 17-12 Magners final triumph over a tired-looking Leinster outfit represented redemption for the Swansea-based region.

The Ospreys, who had come second to Leinster in the league table (52 points to 55), were good on that sunny evening in the Irish capital. Byrne and Bowe scored tries, with Dan Biggar adding points from the boot. A tasty Heineken pool lies ahead including Munster and London Irish. Sadly Gavin Henson cuts a diminished figure these days, at least physically. Having grown frustrated by injury, and seemingly with off-the-field issues to confront as well, he took what was described as 'unpaid leave' before the season was very old, and did not appear for summer training ahead of the 2010-11 season.

The Blues had taken the EDF Energy Cup a year earlier. That it was not the most prestigious competition was offset by the manner of their crushing 50-12 win against Gloucester at Twickenham. Likewise last term. The Amlin Challenge Cup is not the place to be if your ambition is to forge a path to the final stages off the Heineken. However, when you beat Wasps 18-15 on their home pitch in a horrid, wet semi-final, and then are forced to travel down to Marseille to beat the expensively assembled Toulon 28-21 in their own corner of France in temperatures so high as to be infrequent even on the best midsummer's day at Barry Island, that is an achievement Dai Young's team can be proud of.

BELOW Leigh Halfpenny scores for the Blues as they defeat Wasps at Adams Park in the semi-finals of the Amlin Challenge Cup.

FACING PAGE Dan Biggar and Marty Holah of Ospreys celebrate at the final whistle of the inaugural Magners League Grand Final, which the Welsh side won 17-12.

Led by the incomparable Gethin Jenkins (one of several whose summer involved surgery to cure chronic injury) in the absence of Paul Tito, Leigh Halfpenny (who is turning into a very impressive player indeed), Jamie Roberts (another with a surgical appointment) and Bradley Davies (the best young second-row in these islands) scored tries. It was the region's most significant result to date.

Looking ahead, Casey Laulala will be a key figure in midfield, probably in early-season harness with the veteran Tom Shanklin (he's had that description coming for a few years now). A key addition is the Scotland out-half Dan Parks, whose recruitment initially raised eyebrows until the Sydney-born pivot turned out to be one of the players of last year's Six Nations. He will provide a controlling element behind the scrum that the departed Sam Norton-Knight could not. Yet another Kiwi is coming to Cardiff, too – Hurricanes forward Michael Paterson.

Dai Young has stressed the Magners as a priority this time around, the Blues having missed the play-offs with fifth place: 'I don't think we have started well enough in the past.' He welcomed the decision of Xavier Rush to shelve a move to Ulster, especially as golf-buggy driver Andy Powell is heading on up the M4 to Wasps. A Heineken pool containing Castres, Edinburgh and Northampton looks like one the Blues can top.

Paul Turner's coaching team at Newport was joined by an interesting character last season. Colin Charvis retained his individualist approach to the game as his playing career reached its end in an increasingly monochrome era. Now he has won the respect of some experienced Kiwis alongside a spread of promising Welsh talent at Rodney Parade in his new role of forwards coach. A comfortable mid-table position (seventh) was promoted by a strong home record: only the Scarlets and Blues left Gwent as winners in the league.

Alas, the Dragons found the Heineken tough, coming bottom of the group Biarritz won; they have drawn Toulouse next time around. Inevitably, as results improve, international recognition follows. Jason Tovey is not far from the Welsh out-half berth, his left-footedness providing a fresh option to Warren Gatland. Will Harries was capped as a replacement wing against New Zealand in June.

Open-side Robin Sowden-Taylor is a useful recruit from the Blues, along with back-five forward Scott Morgan. Matt Evans, a Canadian international who shone in the 15 and 10 jerseys in the recent Churchill Cup, is an exciting addition. Spare a thought, though, for former captain Michael Owen. The skilful No. 8, a Pontypridd product, who led Wales to the 2005 Grand Slam win over Ireland, was forced to finish his injury-hit career at the end of Saracens' season. Another of his ilk would nicely oil the attacking machine Turner and Charvis are putting together. The leadership of Tom Willis and Luke Charteris will continue to be crucial.

The Scarlets were faced with a Euro-free fixture list had the Blues not triumphed against Toulon. Only Connacht finished below them in the Magners. That is a humbling assessment of where the once-mighty regional team have fallen to. Happily there is realism about their plight, and what needs to be done. A Heineken group containing Perpignan and Leicester is quite a challenge, but doing the double over London Irish last season shows what can be achieved.

Problems are as much off the field as on it. Their filed accounts show a £3.3-million loss, and crowds at the new Parc y Scarlets (itself £4 million over budget) are a third down on estimates at the time the region left Stradey. The chief executive recruited only a year earlier, with experience at the Millennium Stadium, has departed, to be replaced by a man from Honda. How long the patience – and thus investment – of chairman Huw Evans will last is a key question that exercises supporters. Harsh economic times ahead in an area of low population and commercial base do not bode well.

Australian World Cup defence coach John Muggleton has left, but Nigel Davies and forwards coach Simon Easterby remain in charge of the turnaround. They fought hard to retain the iconic figure of Carmarthen's Stephen Jones, despite salary concerns. The bright side is provided by young players who have already featured at national level: Jonathan Davies, Tavis Knoyle, Rob McCusker and hooker Ken Owens, who may turn out to be the best of the lot.

Ireland: No Longer a Minority Sport
by SEAN DIFFLEY

'Meanwhile, in the senior club competition, a splendid final of the AIB League first division saw Cork Constitution snatch a very late winning try through Cronan Healy, in extra time'

After the triumphant 2008-09 season with a Six Nations Grand Slam, a Leinster success in the Heineken Cup and Munster doing their stuff in the Magners League, the past season of 2009-10 brought Irish rugby down to earth. Of course the same two provinces getting to the semifinals of the Heineken Cup and taking on the French sides was really not half bad, and in times of yore would have ranked high amongst the household gods. Indeed, in a small country with limited resources compared with its mightier rivals, it signalled what is now fully accepted in Ireland – that rugby in the Emerald Isle is no longer a minority sport.

On a bright, sunny May day, the new and grandiose Lansdowne Road was officially opened to gasps of astonishment, to be known now,

> **BELOW** The new Lansdowne Road, the Aviva Stadium, opened in May 2010.

LEFT Tommy Bowe of the Ospreys waves to the crowd after the 17-12 Magners League Grand Final defeat of Leinster. It was a tremendous season for the Ireland wing, as he was Players' Player of the Year in both Ireland and Wales, as well as Player of the Championship in the Six Nations.

FACING PAGE Cork Con's Cronan Healy breaks clear of the St Mary's defence during the AIB League division one final. Healy would go on to score the match-winning try in extra time.

in the rarefied sponsorship areas, as the Aviva Stadium. It replaces the old ground, the oldest in international rugby, harking back to the 1870s; a ground that had very much shown its age. The new stadium, a 51,000-capacity all-seater luxury ground, was designed by Populous, a company which has been involved in projects such as Arsenal's Emirates Stadium and the redevelopment of the All England Lawn Tennis Club at Wimbledon and is now engrossed in facilities for the 2012 London Olympics. So, after 132 years of famous matches, success and failure, it is, perhaps, not inappropriate to quote the words of the poet W. B. Yeats, 'A terrible beauty is born', even if Yeats meant something else – anyway, he was born nearby.

As for the Heineken semi-finals, Leinster and Munster succumbed respectively to the great power of Toulouse and Biarritz, who provided a classic lesson in the importance of producing physical power up front. True, both Irish teams lacked some mainstay players due to injuries. Paul O'Connell, for instance, played little during the season because of a groin problem and so Munster were without one of the best locks in world rugby. But, really, there could be no excuses. Toulouse, in particular, virtually pushed the Leinster pack into the Atlantic. The French didn't bother to score tries and used their place-kickers to punish the Irish very effectively in their 26-16 victory. Biarritz, too, in San Sebastián, pummelled the Munster scrum, and if they weren't as impressive or as effective as Toulouse had been the previous day, they were good enough to see off Munster 18-7. And so it was an all-French final in Paris and a clear indication to all the other countries that France have powerful howitzers in store for the World Cup; with defences proving difficult to prise open in midfield, the World Cup will see a concentration of the physical battle, and the French are the first in the northern hemisphere to realise that.

The final of the Magners League, played at the Royal Dublin Society ground, had the Ospreys coming to the Irish capital having last won there back in 2005. But they gave a star performance and were much better than their winning score of 17-12 would indicate. Jonathan Sexton kicked four penalties for Leinster, but Ospreys tries came from Tommy Bowe and Lee Byrne and that was the obvious difference in style and class. The Ospreys tries were vintage stuff and a frantic Leinster could not pierce the Welsh side's defence. Lee Byrne was adjudged man of the match, though many would have preferred the honour to be bestowed on Tommy Bowe, who had a marvellous season and was named Players' Player of the Year in both Ireland and Wales.

That Magners Cup final was Leinster coach Michael Cheika's final match in charge before departing for his new post with Stade Français. The Australian had been five years with the province and his tour of duty turned a famously inconsistent Leinster into better battlers. Before Cheika's arrival in Dublin, Leinster were invariably playing second fiddle to Munster, but in his final season Cheika turned that around, and with his number two, Alan Gaffney, leaving Leinster as well to confine his coaching to the Irish national team, there is an obvious void looming for the Dublin side.

Meanwhile, in the senior club competition, a splendid final of the AIB League first division saw Cork Constitution snatch a very late winning try through Cronan Healy, in extra time, to defeat St Mary's College 17-10. And to end on an ominous note, it was a former St Mary's star – the flying Irish wing, now retired, Denis Hickie – who voiced the concerns in the professional code of rumours that the IRFU were considering pay cuts. The ruling body, which pays the contracted players (unlike in England, where the clubs are the owners), have managed to keep the top players like Brian O'Driscoll at home. But there are stories doing the rounds now that when the contracts come up for renewal soon, there will be cuts, some believing that the reductions could be 50 per cent.

Hickie, no longer a professional footballer, speaks out and says, 'It has taken years to develop Irish rugby but in a year or two it could fall apart. There is no doubt that Irish guys will go abroad if asked to take massive cuts of 30 to 40 per cent or even higher. They can get on a plane for an hour, go to the south of France, play Heineken Cup rugby, get a bigger salary and still be eligible to play for their country.' There are also rumours that the IRFU intends to reduce the number of contracted players from 30 to 21.

YOU'RE IN SAFE HANDS

Wishing Wooden Spoon every success

 INSURANCE 💜 PENSIONS INVESTMENTS

France: From Heroes to Zeros

by CHRIS THAU

'In the middle of all this, the French Championship final brought together the eternal underachievers from Clermont-Ferrand and the reigning champions Perpignan'

With a ninth Grand Slam safely tucked under France's belt and the presence of three of the nation's leading clubs – Toulouse, Biarritz and Toulon – in the finals of the European club competitions, everything seemed to be working well in French rugby, with some self-indulgent comment placing Les Bleus among the favourites in next year's RWC in New Zealand. But a few months later, following a dismal summer tour to South Africa and Argentina during which France suffered two earth-shattering defeats, at the hands of the Springboks (42-17) and the Pumas (41-13), the enthusiasm generated by the winter's results has dissipated. French coach Marc Lièvremont

BELOW Argentina fly half and captain Felipe Contepomi, who plays his rugby at French club Toulon, tormented France in Buenos Aires in June, scoring 31 points – two tries, three conversions and five penalties, in the Pumas' 41-13 win.

and his team are under scrutiny, the players are being criticised for lack of professionalism and the FFR is in the firing line.

This is not the usual French media strop that accompanies a poor campaign. It is more than that and has been brewing in the aftermath of the seemingly successful winter season. It has been argued that the summer Test disaster was waiting to happen, and that action is urgently needed to stop the rot. Seasoned French observers pointed out that the coaching team of Lièvremont, Emile Ntamack and co. is vastly inexperienced and that France play a hybrid game manufactured in the 'Marcoussis laboratories' of the National Rugby Centre, rather than apply the pragmatic approaches developed by highly successful club coaches. They ironically comment that until the 1960s Marcoussis, a market town south of Paris, had supplied the French capital with strawberries and tomatoes, replaced now by rugby dogma and principles. The press point out that the most experienced and successful coaches are working in the club environment – Guy Novès at Toulouse, Vern Cotter at Clermont Auvergne and Philippe Saint-André at Toulon – and that they have been hardly consulted or asked for advice.

In addition, the press say, the players are spoilt and have seemingly lost the appetite to work hard to achieve major goals. They do a job, rather than fulfil a vocation, and this is obvious when they take on southern hemisphere sides, for whom the game is both a profession and more significantly a passion. The players claim that they are tired at the end of a hard season, but the journalists are quick to point out that they do not work hard enough during the season to improve their levels of fitness and comprehension. It has been often said that in the Six Nations, France had in fact flattered to deceive against England and Scotland, both in the middle of a rebuilding process, and against those in mild decline, like Ireland.

In the middle of all this, the occasion of the French Championship final brought together the eternal underachievers from Clermont-Ferrand and the reigning champions Perpignan at Stade de France. With their main kicker Jérôme Porical having a dismal day, Perpignan came to a grinding halt in front of a team inspired by its sense of mission. Clermont finally put the ghosts of their previous failures to rest with a solid performance full of confidence and purpose. On their 11th appearance in the final of the championship, after ten runners-up medals between 1936 and 2009, the men of Auvergne finally took home the coveted Bouclier de Brennus. Head coach Vern Cotter, his right-hand man Joe Schmidt on his final assignment with the club, and captain Aurélien Rougerie led the procession in Clermont-Ferrand's main square, Place de Jaude, greeted by 30,000 ecstatic supporters. 'It was well deserved,' observed Jean-Roger Delsaud, editor of *Midi Olympique*, the voice of French rugby. 'However, this is the end of an era for Clermont and the beginning of a new one. Montferrand will no longer be treated as the darlings of French rugby. Now they are champions and have now graduated among the big boys. Everybody will target them, will want to beat them. From now on their life will be different,' he added.

Earlier, the Real Madrid of rugby football, Stade Toulousain, defeated Biarritz 21-19 to win their fourth Heineken Cup in six final appearances – an outstanding record by any measure. Knocked out of the French Championship by Perpignan, Toulouse put all their resources into the Heineken Cup, making a great statement about the perennial values that have inspired them during a century of success.

BELOW Clermont Auvergne lay hold of the Bouclier de Brennus, having won the French Championship final for the first time at the 11th attempt.

FACING PAGE Clermont's Napolioni Nalaga, who scored the only try of the final, is stopped short this time by the Perpignan defence.

Italy: All Change in 2010-11
by CHRIS THAU

'But this was only the beginning of a year-long political battle, which ended up with Treviso back in the fold at the expense of Parma and Viadana replacing Rome'

Without a doubt, the offer of the Magners League to accommodate two Italian teams has been the most significant development in Italian rugby since they joined the Six Nations ten years ago. However, as in all things in Italian rugby, choosing the two clubs was a fairly laborious affair, with considerable implications, which explained the various combinations put forward at one time or another. Last year when the announcement was first made, the two teams mentioned were a Parma-based selection, to be baptised Aironi, and a Roman team, under the name of Praetorians. That would have left Veneto, historically the most productive Italian rugby nursery, and its leading club Treviso out in the wilderness.

But this was only the beginning of a year-long political battle, which ended up with Treviso back in the fold at the expense of Parma and Viadana replacing Rome as the second Italian super club. Treviso will

BELOW Treviso prop Lorenzo Cittadini is tackled by Viadana's fly half Mark Woodrow during the 2010 Super 10 final in Padua. Both sides have now left the Italian Championship to take part in the Magners League.

maintain its name Benetton for obvious reasons, while Viadana will operate under the name of Aironi, with the still-born Praetorians confined to the dustbin of Italian rugby history. All this has had in it an element of poetic justice as the two elected clubs reached, once again, the final of the Italian Super 10.

In the semi-finals, played on a home-and-away basis, Montepaschi Viadana managed to overcome Femi-Cz Rovigo on aggregate, winning the home leg 25-16, thanks to a five-penalty spree in the second half by full back Garry Law, while losing 18-22 at Rovigo, with Law again the main points scorer. One of the by-products of the defeat of Rovigo was the demise of their capable coach, Umberto Casellato, a former Italy scrum half. In the other semi-final, Treviso triumphed over Petrarca Padova, winning the away leg 28-16 followed by a 54-10 demolition at home.

In the final at the end of May, Treviso, coached by South African Franco Smith, nudged ahead of Franco Bernini's Viadana, thanks to a try by wing Andrew Vilk, to win 16-12 and claim their 15th championship title. Next season Treviso and Viadana will be replaced by Lazio and Mogliano, with the long-term future of Super 10 in its present format somewhat in doubt.

The realignment process in Italian rugby, which has already seen the disappearance from the professional ranks of Calvisano, one of the great Italian clubs of the past two decades, has only commenced. While Treviso and Viadana will go from strength to strength, the remainder of the Italian senior clubs are likely to struggle, with the merger of Parma with the neighbouring Noceto club this season's notable event.

Meanwhile, Smith and Bernini, the coaches of Treviso and Viadana respectively, will carry on, their futures dependent very much on the performances of the two clubs in Europe. Naturally this will be dictated to an extent by their coaching ability but more significantly by their transfer budgets. At this stage it is known that the budgets of both Benetton and Aironi will match those of the Irish, Scottish and Welsh provincial teams, which does not necessarily mean that the quality of their foreign imports will go up. The two clubs have been targeted by the Italian Federation (FIR) for their ability to provide top Italian players with a stepping stone to the dizzying heights of international rugby, not for their ability to attract foreign stars.

In this respect the key to the entire package is the announcement that FIR will cover 50 per cent of their budgets, a commitment that will prevent both Treviso and Viadana from employing more than five players ineligible to play for Italy. In the short term this clearly makes current Italian internationals a highly desired commodity, while in the long term it will obviously lead to a concentration of quality Italian players at the two clubs. The latter process has already commenced, with the announcement that both Salvatore Perugini and Marco Bortolami will be returning to Italy to join Viadana, a move expected to be emulated by more of the 20-odd Italian expatriates. But not all of them will follow suit, since the salaries of the big French and English clubs remain a strong incentive for the Italian superstars of the likes of Sergio Parisse, the captain of Stade Français, and Mirco Bergamasco, who left his brother Mauro behind at Stade to join Parisian rivals Racing Métro 92.

While the 50 per cent stake in the two clubs will not necessarily grant Italy coach Nick Mallett and his assistants Alex Troncon and Carlo Orlandi a say in their recruitment policy, the stated aim of upgrading the quality of Italian players reaching the national team remains the main objective. At development level, the overhaul of Italian rugby will commence when Craig Green, the former All Black player and Treviso coach, takes over the position of development director in the footsteps of the retired Frenchman Georges Coste. Coste, a former Italy national coach, has done a marvellous job, but Italy are still unable to bridge the gap at age-group level, which is ultimately reflected in the performance of the national team.

The summer Test series against South Africa is evidence of this gap. In the First Test, with the South African team out of sorts and the Italians playing little rugby, the losing margin was only 16 points (29-13) – the smallest between the two nations – with the Italians missing a huge opportunity to score a try in the closing stages of a forgettable Test. It is quite clear that Italy have made tremendous progress since they were annihilated 101-0 by the Springboks in the build-up to RWC 1999, when a players' revolt forced the then coach Georges Coste to step down. In the Second Test in East London, with the Italian scrummage in tatters and their back row and backs making a cacophony of defensive errors, the balance was re-established, with the Boks scoring seven tries to win 55-11 in a match in which Italy at least tried to play rugby.

A Summary of the Season 2009-10

by TERRY COOPER

INTERNATIONAL RUGBY

AUSTRALIA TO BRITISH ISLES
NOVEMBER 2009

Opponents	Results
Gloucester	W 36-5
ENGLAND	W 18-9
IRELAND	D 20-20
SCOTLAND	L 8-9
Cardiff	W 31-3
WALES	W 33-12

Played 6 Won 4 Drawn 1 Lost 1

NEW ZEALAND TO EUROPE
NOVEMBER 2009

Opponents	Results
WALES	W 19-12
ITALY	W 20-6
ENGLAND	W 19-6
FRANCE	W 39-12
Barbarians	L 18-25

Played 5 Won 4 Lost 1

SOUTH AFRICA TO EUROPE
NOVEMBER 2009

Opponents	Results
Leicester	L 17-22
FRANCE	L 13-20
Saracens	L 23-24
ITALY	W 32-10
IRELAND	L 10-15

Played 5 Won 1 Lost 4

SAMOA TO EUROPE
NOVEMBER 2009

Opponents	Results
WALES	L 13-17
FRANCE	L 5-43
ITALY	L 6-24

Played 3 Lost 3

FIJI TO EUROPE
NOVEMBER 2009

Opponents	Results
SCOTLAND	L 10-23
IRELAND	L 6-41
ROMANIA	W 29-18

Played 3 Won 1 Lost 2

ARGENTINA TO UNITED KINGDOM
NOVEMBER 2009

Opponents	Results
ENGLAND	L 9-16
WALES	L 16-33
SCOTLAND	W 9-6

Played 3 Won 1 Lost 2

ENGLAND TO AUSTRALIA & NEW ZEALAND
JUNE 2010

Opponents	Results
Australian Barbarians	D 28-28
AUSTRALIA	L 17-27
Australian Barbarians	W 15-9
AUSTRALIA	W 21-20
New Zealand Maori	L 28-35

Played 5 Won 2 Drawn 1 Lost 2

IRELAND TO NEW ZEALAND & AUSTRALIA
JUNE 2010

Opponents	Results
NEW ZEALAND	L 28-66
New Zealand Maori	L 28-31
AUSTRALIA	L 15-22

Played 3 Lost 3

WALES TO NEW ZEALAND
JUNE 2010

Opponents	Results
NEW ZEALAND	L 9-42
NEW ZEALAND	L 10-29

Played 2 Lost 2

SCOTLAND TO ARGENTINA
JUNE 2010

Opponents	Results
ARGENTINA	W 24-16
ARGENTINA	W 13-9

Played 2 Won 2

ITALY TO SOUTH AFRICA
JUNE 2010

Opponents	Results
SOUTH AFRICA	L 13-29
SOUTH AFRICA	L 11-55

Played 2 Lost 2

FRANCE TO SOUTH AFRICA & ARGENTINA
JUNE 2010

Opponents	Results
SOUTH AFRICA	L 17-42
Argentine Select XV	W 37-14
ARGENTINA	L 13-41

Played 3 Won 1 Lost 2

OTHER INTERNATIONAL MATCHES

Australia	19	New Zealand	32
	(Bledisloe Cup; held in Tokyo)		
Japan	46	Canada	8
Japan	27	Canada	6
Portugal	19	Tonga	24
Canada	22	Russia	6
Wales	31	South Africa	34

ROYAL BANK OF SCOTLAND
SIX NATIONS CHAMPIONSHIP 2010

Results

Ireland	29	Italy	11
England	30	Wales	17
Scotland	9	France	18
Wales	31	Scotland	24
France	33	Ireland	10
Italy	12	England	17
Wales	20	France	26
Italy	16	Scotland	12
England	16	Ireland	20
Ireland	27	Wales	12
Scotland	15	England	15
France	46	Italy	20
Wales	33	Italy	10
Ireland	20	Scotland	23
France	12	England	10

Final table

	P	W	D	L	F	A	PD	Pts
France	5	5	0	0	135	69	66	10
Ireland	5	3	0	2	106	95	11	6
England	5	2	1	2	88	76	12	5
Wales	5	2	0	3	113	117	-4	4
Scotland	5	1	1	3	83	100	-17	3
Italy	5	1	0	4	69	137	-68	2

UNDER 20 SIX NATIONS 2010

Results

Scotland	8	France	8
Ireland	39	Italy	0
England	41	Wales	14
Italy	10	England	16
Wales	20	Scotland	12
France	20	Ireland	15
Wales	43	France	8
Italy	16	Scotland	18
England	10	Ireland	25
Scotland	6	England	27
Ireland	24	Wales	17
France	25	Italy	6
Ireland	44	Scotland	15
Wales	30	Italy	22
France	33	England	47

Final table

	P	W	D	L	F	A	PD	Pts
Ireland	5	4	0	1	147	62	85	8
England	5	4	0	1	141	88	53	8
Wales	5	3	0	2	124	107	17	6
France	5	2	1	2	94	119	-25	5
Scotland	5	1	1	3	59	115	-56	3
Italy	5	0	0	5	54	128	-74	0

WOMEN'S SIX NATIONS 2010

Results

Ireland	22	Italy	5
England	31	Wales	0
Scotland	10	France	8
France	19	Ireland	9
Italy	0	England	41
Wales	28	Scotland	12
Wales	3	France	15
Italy	6	Scotland	6
England	22	Ireland	5
Ireland	18	Wales	3
Scotland	0	England	51
France	45	Italy	14
Ireland	15	Scotland	3
France	10	England	11
Wales	15	Italy	19

Final table

	P	W	D	L	F	A	PD	Pts
England	5	5	0	0	156	15	141	10
France	5	3	0	2	97	47	50	6
Ireland	5	3	0	2	69	52	17	6
Scotland	5	1	1	3	31	108	77	3
Italy	5	1	1	3	44	129	85	3
Wales	5	1	0	4	49	95	46	2

LAGER. BURP. SERVED SUPER-CHILLED TO HIDE THE TASTE. BURP. AS UBIQUITOUS AS THE COMMON COLD. BURP. AND JUST AS ENJOYABLE. BURP. LOOKS THE SAME COMING OUT AS IT DOES GOING IN. BURP. OH, AND IT'S GASSY. BURP.

GREENE KING IPA

BREWING PERFECTION

THE PINT
WITH NOTHING
TO PROVE

OFFICIAL BEER OF
ENGLAND
RUGBY

ENGLAND
RUGBY

greenekingipa.co.uk

UNDER 18 SIX NATIONS FESTIVAL 2010

(Held in April in Llandovery, Wales)

Results

Ireland	18	Wales	24
Scotland	5	England	32
England	41	Ireland	17
Scotland	33	Italy	13
Wales	94	Italy	3
Scotland	24	Ireland	28

TRI-NATIONS 2009

Results

New Zealand	22	Australia	16
South Africa	28	New Zealand	19
South Africa	31	New Zealand	19
South Africa	29	Australia	17
Australia	18	New Zealand	19
Australia	25	South Africa	32
Australia	21	South Africa	6
New Zealand	29	South Africa	32
New Zealand	33	Australia	6

Champions: South Africa

TRI-NATIONS 2010 (to date)

Results

New Zealand	32	South Africa	12
New Zealand	31	South Africa	17
Australia	30	South Africa	13
Australia	28	New Zealand	49
New Zealand	20	Australia	10
South Africa	22	New Zealand	29
South Africa	44	Australia	31

IRB PACIFIC NATIONS CUP 2010

Results

Samoa	24	Tonga	23
Fiji	22	Japan	8
Samoa	23	Japan	31
Fiji	41	Tonga	38
Fiji	9	Samoa	31
Japan	26	Tonga	23

Champions: Samoa

CHURCHILL CUP 2010

(Held in June in Glendale, Colorado, and Harrison, New Jersey, USA)

Pool A

Canada	33	France A	27
France A	43	Uruguay	10
Canada	48	Uruguay	6

Pool B

USA	9	England Saxons	32
England Saxons	49	Russia	17
Russia	22	USA	39

Bowl Final

Russia	38	Uruguay	19

Plate Final

France A	24	USA	10

Cup Final

Canada	18	England Saxons	38

IRB NATIONS CUP 2010

(Held in June in Bucharest, Romania)

Namibia	21	Romania	17
Argentina Jaguars	20	Italy A	22
Scotland A	21	Georgia	22
Italy A	21	Georgia	3
Scotland A	20	Namibia	23
Romania	24	Argentina Jaguars	8
Georgia	16	Namibia	21
Argentina Jaguars	33	Scotland A	13
Italy A	22	Romania	27

Champions: Namibia

IRB JUNIOR WORLD CHAMPIONSHIP 2010

(Held in June in Argentina)

Semi-finals

Australia	28	England	16
New Zealand	36	South Africa	7

Final

New Zealand	62	Australia	17

IRB JUNIOR WORLD RUGBY TROPHY 2010

(Held in June in Russia)

Third-place Play-off

Russia	23	Romania	20

Final

Italy	36	Japan	7

IRB SEVENS WORLD SERIES FINALS 2009-10

Dubai

New Zealand	24	Samoa	12

South Africa (George)

New Zealand	21	Fiji	12

New Zealand (Wellington)

Fiji	19	Samoa	14

United States (Las Vegas)

Samoa	33	New Zealand	12

Australia (Adelaide)

Samoa	38	USA	10

Hong Kong

Samoa	24	New Zealand	21

England (Twickenham)

Australia	19	South Africa	14

Scotland (Murrayfield)

Samoa	41	Australia	14

IRB Sevens Champions: Samoa

CLUB, COUNTY AND DIVISIONAL RUGBY

ENGLAND

Guinness Premiership

	P	W	D	L	F	A	BP	Pts
Leicester	22	15	1	6	541	325	11	73
Northampton	22	16	0	6	472	322	7	71
Saracens	22	15	1	6	480	367	7	69
Bath	22	12	2	8	450	366	9	61
Wasps	22	13	0	9	394	399	5	57
London Irish	22	10	3	9	469	384	6	52
Gloucester	22	10	1	11	470	457	6	48
Harlequins	22	9	2	11	420	484	6	46
Newcastle	22	6	4	12	319	431	5	37
Leeds	22	7	1	14	283	493	6	36
Sale	22	6	1	15	333	495	6	32
Worcester	22	3	4	15	312	420	8	28

Relegated: Worcester

Guinness Premiership Play-offs
Semi-finals

Northampton	19	Saracens	21
Leicester	15	Bath	6

Final

Leicester	33	Saracens	27

RFU Championship
Division Winners: Bristol
Division Runners-up: Exeter

RFU Championship Play-offs Final

Exeter	9	Bristol	6
Bristol	10	Exeter	29

Promoted to Premiership: Exeter

National Leagues
National 1 Champions: Esher
Runners-up: London Scottish
National 2 (S) Champions: Barking
Runners-up: Rosslyn Park
National 2 (N) Champions: Macclesfield
Runners-up: Loughborough Students

RFU League Champions Cup Finals
National 2

Macclesfield	30	Barking	26

National 3

Ampthill	12	Jersey	21

Divisional 1

Scunthorpe	10	Hartpury College	76

RFU Knockout Trophy Finals
Intermediate Cup

Old Redcliffians	42	Northern	21

Senior Vase

Brighton	32	Dunlop	3

Junior Vase

Teddington	43	Bramley Phoenix	21

National Under 20 Championship Final

Yorkshire	15	Glos	13

County Championships Finals
Bill Beaumont Cup

Lancashire	36	Glos	6

Bill Beaumont Cup Division Two (Plate)

Kent	33	Warwickshire	27

County Championship Shield

Dorset & Wilts	36	Leicestershire	26

Oxbridge University Matches
Varsity Match

Cambridge	31	Oxford	27

Under 21 Varsity Match

Oxford	53	Cambridge	17

Women's Varsity Match

Cambridge	25	Oxford	0

BUCS Competitions
Men's Championship Winners: Loughborough
Women's Championship Winners: UWIC
Men's Trophy Winners: Loughborough
Women's Trophy Winners: Bath

Inter-Services Champions: Royal Navy

Hospitals Cup Winners: Imperial College

Middlesex Sevens 2009
Winners: London Irish
Runners-up: ULR Samurai Internationals

Rosslyn Park Schools Sevens
Open Winners: Millfield
Festival Winners: Tonbridge
Colts Winners: Millfield
Preparatory Winners: Millfield
Juniors Winners: Wimbledon
Girls Winners: Hartpury College

Daily Mail Schools Day
Under 18 Cup Winners: Whitgift
Under 18 Vase Winners: Sandbach
Under 15 Cup Winners: Wilmslow HS
Under 15 Vase Winners: Lymm HS

Women's Premiership Champions: Richmond

SCOTLAND

Scottish Hydro Premier Cup Final
Ayr 36 Melrose 23
Scottish Hydro National Shield Final
Lasswade 17 Greenock Wdrs 7
Scottish Hydro Regional Bowl Final
North Berwick 13 Strathmore 8

Scottish Sevens Winners
Kelso: Melrose
Selkirk: Selkirk
Melrose: Hamilton
Hawick: Hawick
Berwick: Selkirk
Langholm: Kelso
Peebles: Melrose
Gala: Melrose
Earlston: Melrose
Jed-Forest: Melrose
Kings of the Sevens: Melrose

Scottish Hydro Premiership
Division 1

	P	W	D	L	F	A	BP	Pts
Currie	22	21	0	1	952	318	17	101
*Ayr	21	19	0	2	667	362	16	92
Melrose	22	12	2	8	600	453	15	67
Dundee	22	12	0	10	587	454	15	63
Heriot's	22	12	0	10	580	496	12	60
Glasgow Hawks	22	12	1	9	576	521	10	60
*Selkirk	21	8	2	11	488	633	8	44
Boroughmuir	22	8	0	14	467	599	11	43
W of Scotland	22	8	0	14	475	697	11	43
Watsonians	22	7	1	14	393	578	9	39
Edinburgh Acads	22	7	0	15	421	569	9	37
Stewart's Melville	22	2	0	20	323	849	5	13

*Ayr and Selkirk agreed not to fulfil their final fixture because of fixture congestion. Final league placings were not affected.

Champions: Currie
Relegated: Edinburgh Acads, Stewart's Melville

Division 2

	P	W	D	L	F	A	BP	Pts
Stirling County	22	18	0	4	685	301	18	90
Hawick	22	18	1	3	592	359	10	84
Gala	22	14	0	8	441	327	10	66
Biggar	22	13	1	8	463	353	8	62
GHA	22	11	2	9	529	487	9	57
Aberdeen GSFP	22	11	0	11	539	438	12	56
Kirkcaldy	22	10	0	12	500	475	12	52
Peebles	22	9	0	13	414	414	13	49
Kelso	22	10	0	12	388	399	8	48
Jed-Forest	22	6	2	14	399	537	5	33
Haddington	22	4	2	16	295	663	3	23
Dunfermline	22	4	0	18	283	775	6	22

Champions: Stirling County
Also promoted: Hawick
Relegated: Haddington, Dunfermline

WALES

SWALEC Cup
Semi-finals
Carmarthen 41 Pontypridd 12
Llanelli 46 Cardiff 25

Final
Carmarthen 8 Llanelli 20

SWALEC Plate Final
Kenfig Hill 25 Maesteg 33

SWALEC Bowl Final
Abercarn 39 Trebanos 3

Principality Premiership

	P	W	D	L	F	A	BP	Pts
Neath	26	21	0	5	927	532	20	104
Swansea	26	19	1	6	780	527	18	96
Newport	26	18	0	8	685	470	14	86
Pontypridd	26	16	1	9	682	486	15	81
Aberavon	26	14	4	8	709	617	13	77
Llanelli	26	14	2	10	663	565	17	77
Cardiff	26	15	2	9	612	507	11	75
Llandovery	26	12	1	13	636	621	10	60
Carmarthen	26	11	0	15	515	562	8	52
Cross Keys	26	9	1	16	502	550	9	47
Bedwas	26	8	0	18	516	792	12	44
The Wanderers	26	7	0	19	461	657	12	40
Pontypool	26	7	0	19	464	891	8	36
Ebbw Vale	26	5	0	21	312	687	8	28

SWALEC Leagues
Division 1 East

	P	W	D	L	F	A	BP	Pts
UWIC	22	19	0	3	636	276	12	88
Llanharan	22	17	0	5	697	383	16	84
Blackwood	22	16	0	6	616	333	13	77
Bargoed	22	16	0	6	624	408	12	76
Newbridge	22	13	0	9	457	464	9	61
Rumney	22	10	0	12	460	522	8	48
Bedlinog	22	9	0	13	344	415	5	41
Merthyr	22	7	1	14	453	548	10	40
Ystrad Rhondda	22	7	0	15	421	622	9	37
Beddau	22	7	1	14	341	501	7	37
Tredegar	22	7	0	15	374	570	8	36
Caerphilly	22	3	0	19	314	695	6	18

Division 1 West

	P	W	D	L	F	A	BP	Pts
Tonmawr	22	20	0	2	714	269	15	95
Whitland	22	13	2	7	449	330	10	66
Corus (P Talbot)	22	12	1	9	496	450	9	59
Boymaen	22	12	0	10	477	372	11	59
Bridgend Ath	22	12	1	9	413	415	8	58
Narberth	22	11	0	11	407	445	10	54
Felinfoel	22	11	0	11	402	563	6	50
Llangennech	22	11	0	11	410	431	6	50
Bridgend	22	8	1	13	448	442	12	46
Carmarthen Ath	22	9	0	13	398	436	9	45
Builth Wells	22	7	1	14	412	583	7	37
Cwmllynfell	22	3	0	19	360	650	5	17

IRELAND

AIB League
Division 1A

	P	W	D	L	F	A	BP	Pts
Cork Const'n	14	10	1	3	231	165	4	46
St Mary's College	14	9	0	5	286	200	7	43
Dolphin	14	8	0	6	225	202	4	36
Blackrock College	14	7	0	7	235	207	6	34
Shannon	14	6	0	8	242	218	10	34
Garryowen	14	7	1	6	158	201	4	34
Clontarf	14	5	0	9	214	257	4	24
UL Bohemian	14	3	0	11	149	290	4	16

Division 1B

	P	W	D	L	F	A	BP	Pts
Old Belvedere	14	11	1	2	398	166	10	56
Young Munster	14	11	1	2	224	138	2	48
UCC	14	7	0	7	228	220	5	33
Galwegians	14	6	0	8	180	244	5	29
Buccaneers	14	6	0	8	175	254	3	27
Dungannon	14	5	0	9	192	245	6	26
Ballymena	14	5	0	9	228	287	4	24
Ballynahinch	14	4	0	10	239	310	8	24

AIB League Play-offs
Division 1
Semi-finals

St Mary's Coll	24	Old Belvedere	23
Cork Constitution	31	Dolphin	18

Final

Cork Constitution	17	St Mary's Coll	10

Division 2
Division Winners: Lansdowne
Play-off Champions: Lansdowne
Play-off Runners-up: Bruff

Division 3
Division Winners: Queens University
Play-off Champions: Queens University
Play-off Runners-up: Nenagh Ormond

AIB Cup

Cork Constitution	15	Garryowen	11

AIB Junior Cup

Armagh	17	City of Derry	19

All Ireland Provincial League Champions
Seapoint

Senior Cup Winners
Leinster: St Mary's College
Munster: Young Munster
Ulster: Queens University
Connacht: Corinthians

MAGNERS LEAGUE 2009-10

	P	W	D	L	F	A	BP	Pts
Leinster	18	13	0	5	359	295	3	55
Ospreys	18	11	1	6	384	298	6	52
Warriors	18	11	2	5	390	321	3	51
Munster	18	9	0	9	319	282	9	45
Blues	18	10	0	8	349	315	4	44
Edinburgh	18	8	0	10	385	391	9	41
Dragons	18	8	1	9	333	378	5	39
Ulster	18	7	1	10	357	370	6	36
Scarlets	18	5	0	13	361	382	9	29
Connacht	18	5	1	12	254	459	4	26

Magners League Play-offs
Semi-finals

Ospreys	20	Warriors	5
Leinster	16	Munster	6

Final

Leinster	12	Ospreys	17

LV= CUP 2009-10

Semi-finals

Cardiff Blues	18	Gloucester	29
Northampton	31	Saracens	20

Final

Northampton	30	Gloucester	24

BRITISH & IRISH CUP 2009-10

Final

Cornish Pirates	23	Munster	14

FRANCE

'Top 14' Play-offs

Semi-finals

Perpignan	21	Toulouse	13
Clermont Auvergne	35	Toulon	29

Final

Clermont Auvergne	19	Perpignan	6

ITALY

'Super 10'

Final

Benetton Treviso	16	M/paschi Viadana	12

HEINEKEN CUP 2009-10

Quarter-finals

Leinster	29	Clermont A'gne	28
Munster	33	Northampton	19
Biarritz	29	Ospreys	28
Toulouse	42	Stade Français	16

Semi-finals

Toulouse	26	Leinster	16
Biarritz	18	Munster	7

Final

Biarritz	19	Toulouse	21

AMLIN CHALLENGE CUP 2009-10

Quarter-finals

Connacht	23	Bourgoin	20
Toulon	38	Scarlets	12
Wasps	42	Gloucester	26
Newcastle	20	Cardiff Blues	55

Semi-finals

Connacht	12	Toulon	19
Wasps	15	Cardiff Blues	18

Final

Cardiff Blues	28	Toulon	21

NEW ZEALAND

Air New Zealand Cup 2009

Final

Canterbury	28	Wellington	20

Ranfurly Shield holders: Southland

SOUTH AFRICA

Currie Cup 2009

Final

Blue Bulls	36	FS Cheetahs	24

SUPER 14 TOURNAMENT 2010

Final table

	P	W	D	L	F	A	BP	Pts
Bulls	13	10	0	3	436	345	7	47
Stormers	13	9	0	4	365	171	8	44
Waratahs	13	9	0	4	385	288	7	43
Crusaders	13	8	1	4	388	295	7	41
Reds	13	8	0	5	366	308	7	39
Brumbies	13	8	0	5	358	291	5	37
Blues	13	7	0	6	376	333	9	37
Hurricanes	13	7	1	5	358	323	7	37
Sharks	13	7	0	6	297	299	5	33
Cheetahs	13	5	1	7	316	393	4	26
Chiefs	13	4	1	8	340	418	8	26
Highlanders	13	3	0	10	297	397	7	19
Western Force	13	4	0	9	258	364	3	19
Lions	13	0	0	13	270	585	5	5

Semi-finals

Bulls	39	Crusaders	24
Stormers	25	Waratahs	6

Final

Bulls	25	Stormers	17

BARBARIANS

Opponents	Results
Combined Services	L 19-22
New Zealand	W 25-18
Bedford	L 14-50
England	L 26-35
Ireland	W 29-23

Played 5 Won 2 Lost 3

"Wishing the Wooden Spoon every success with their ongoing work"

PREVIEW OF THE SEASON 2010-11

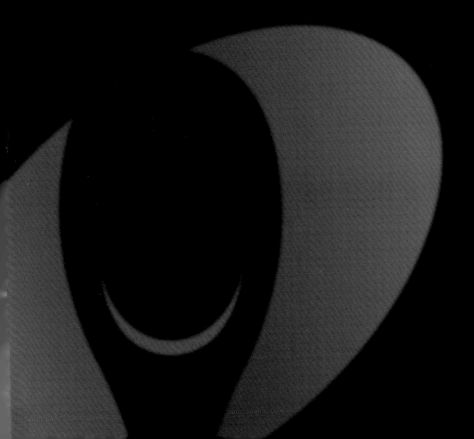

Key Players
selected by IAN ROBERTSON

ENGLAND

BEN FODEN
Northampton Saints
Born: 22 July 1985
Height: 6ft Weight: 14st 9lbs
Full back – 6 caps
1st cap v Italy 2009

DAN COLE
Leicester Tigers
Born: 9 May 1987
Height: 6ft 3ins Weight: 19st 1lb
Prop – 7 caps
1st cap v Wales 2010

SCOTLAND

DAN PARKS
Glasgow Rugby
Born: 26 May 1978
Height: 5ft 11ins Weight: 14st 7lbs
Fly half – 53 caps
1st cap v Wales 2004

JOHN BEATTIE
Glasgow Rugby
Born: 21 November 1985
Height: 6ft 4ins Weight: 16st 10lbs
Back-row – 14 caps
1st cap v Romania 2006

WALES

DAN BIGGAR
Ospreys
Born: 16 October 1989
Height: 6ft Weight: 14st
Fly half – 6 caps
1st cap v Canada 2008

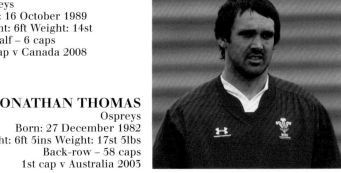

JONATHAN THOMAS
Ospreys
Born: 27 December 1982
Height: 6ft 5ins Weight: 17st 5lbs
Back-row – 58 caps
1st cap v Australia 2003

Six Nations Championship

2010-11

IRELAND

TOMMY BOWE
Ospreys
Born: 22 February 1984
Height: 6ft 3ins Weight: 15st 3lbs
Wing – 32 caps (+3 Lions)
1st cap v USA 2004

STEPHEN FERRIS
Ulster
Born: 2 August 1985
Height: 6ft 4ins Weight: 17st 2lbs
Back-row – 20 caps
1st cap v Pacific Islanders 2006

FRANCE

MORGAN PARRA
ASM Clermont Auvergne
Born: 15 November 1988
Height: 5ft 11ins Weight: 11st 13lbs
Scrum half – 19 caps
1st cap v Scotland 2008

LOUIS PICAMOLES
Stade Toulousain
Born: 5 February 1986
Height: 6ft 4ins Weight: 16st 10lbs
Back-row – 17 caps
1st cap v Ireland 2008

ITALY

GONZALO CANALE
ASM Clermont Auvergne
Born: 11 November 1982
Height: 5ft 11ins Weight: 14st 9lbs
Centre – 58 caps
1st cap v Scotland 2003

ALESSANDRO ZANNI
Benetton Treviso
Born: 31 August 1984
Height: 6ft 4ins Weight: 16st 4lbs
Back-row – 44 caps
1st cap v Tonga 2005

Fixtures 2010-11

AUGUST 2010

Fri. 20th to	
Sun. Sept. 5th	Women's Rugby World Cup
Sat. 21st	Scottish Premiership 1 & 2
Sat. 28th	SA v AUSTRALIA (Tri-Nations)
	Welsh Principality Premiership
	Scottish Premiership 1-3
	Scottish National Leagues 1-3
Sat. 28th and	
Sun. 29th	English National Championship

SEPTEMBER 2010

Fri. 3rd and	
Sat. 4th	Aviva English Premiership
	Magners Celtic League (1)
Sat. 4th	SA v AUSTRALIA (Tri-Nations)
	English National Championship
	English National Leagues
	Scottish Premiership 1-3
	Scottish National Leagues 1-3
	Welsh Principality Premiership
	Swalec Welsh Nat Lges E,W,N
Fri. 10th and	
Sat. 11th	Aviva English Premiership
Fri. 10th to	
Sun. 12th	Magners Celtic League (2)
Sat. 11th	AUSTRALIA v NZ (Tri-Nations)
	English National Leagues
	Scottish Premiership 1-3
	Scottish National Leagues 1-3
	Welsh Principality Premiership
	Swalec Welsh Nat Lges E,W,N
Sat. 11th and	
Sun. 12th	English National Championship
Fri. 17th and	
Sat. 18th	Magners Celtic League (3)
Fri. 17th to	
Sun. 19th	Aviva English Premiership
Sat. 18th	English National Championship
	English National Leagues
	Scottish Premiership 1-3
	Scottish National Leagues 1-3
	Welsh Principality Premiership
	Swalec Welsh Nat Lges E,W,N
Wed. 22nd	Welsh Principality Premiership
Fri. 24th and	
Sat. 25th	English National Championship
	Magners Celtic League (4)
Sat. 25th	English National Leagues
	Scottish Premiership 1-3
	Scottish National Leagues 1-3
	Welsh Principality Premiership
	Swalec Welsh Nat Lges E,W,N
Sat. 25th &	
Sun. 26th	Aviva English Premiership
Thu. 30th to	
Sun. Oct. 3rd	Magners Celtic League (5)

OCTOBER 2010

Fri. 1st and	
Sat. 2nd	English National Championship
Fri. 1st to	
Sun. 3rd	Aviva English Premiership
Sat. 2nd	English National Leagues
	Scottish Premiership 1-3
	Scottish National Leagues 1-3
	Welsh Principality Premiership
	Swalec Welsh Nat Lges E,W,N
	Irish Leagues 1A & B, 2, 3
Thu. 7th to	
Sun. 10th	Amlin Challenge Cup (1)
Fri. 8th to	
Sun. 10th	Heineken Cup (1)
	English National Championship
Sat. 9th	English National Leagues
	Scottish Premiership 1-3
	Scottish National Leagues 1-3
	Welsh Principality Premiership
	Swalec Welsh Nat Lges E & W
	Swalec Bowl (1)
	Irish Leagues 1A & B, 2, 3
Thu. 14th to	
Sun. 17th	Amlin Challenge Cup (2)
Fri. 15th to	
Sun. 17th	Heineken Cup (2)
Sat. 16th	English National Championship
	English National Leagues
	Scottish Premiership 1-3
	Scottish National Leagues 1-3
	Welsh Principality Premiership
	Swalec Welsh Nat Lges E,W,N
	British & Irish Cup (5*)
Fri. 22nd to	
Sun. 24th	Aviva English Premiership
	Magners Celtic League (6)
Sat. 23rd	English National Leagues
	Scottish Premiership 1-3
	Scottish National Leagues 1-3
	Welsh Principality Premiership
	Swalec Welsh Nat Lges E,W,N
	Irish Leagues 1A & B, 3
Sat. 23rd and	
Sun. 24th	English National Championship
	Irish League 2
Fri. 29th and	
Sat. 30th	Magners Celtic League (7)
Sat. 30th	English National Championship
	English National Leagues
	Scottish Premiership 1-3
	Scottish National Leagues 1-3
	Welsh Principality Premiership
	Swalec Welsh Nat Lges E & W
	Swalec Plate (1)
	Swalec Bowl (2)
	Irish Leagues 1A & B, 2, 3

Sat. 30th and	
Sun. 31st	Aviva English Premiership

NOVEMBER 2010

Fri. 5th and	
Sun. 7th	Magners Celtic League (8*)
Sat. 6th	ENGLAND v NEW ZEALAND
	WALES v AUSTRALIA
	IRELAND v SOUTH AFRICA
	LV= (Anglo-Welsh) Cup (1)
	English National Leagues
	Scottish National Leagues 1-3
	Scottish Premier Cup (1)
	Welsh Principality Premiership
	Swalec Welsh Nat Lges E & W
Sat. 6th and	
Sun. 7th	English National Championship
Tue. 9th	Welsh Principality Premiership
Fri. 12th	WALES v SOUTH AFRICA
Fri. 12th and	
Sat. 13th	English National Championship
Sat. 13th	ENGLAND v AUSTRALIA
	SCOTLAND v NEW ZEALAND
	FRANCE v SOUTH AFRICA
	IRELAND v SAMOA
	LV= (Anglo-Welsh) Cup (2)
	English National Leagues
	Scottish Premiership 1 & 2 (tbc)
	Scottish Premiership 3
	Welsh Principality Premiership
Fri. 19th	WALES v FIJI
Fri. 19th and	
Sun. 21st	Magners Celtic League (8*)
Fri. 19th to	
Sun. 21st	Aviva English Premiership
Sat. 20th	ENGLAND v SAMOA
	SCOTLAND v SOUTH AFRICA
	IRELAND v NEW ZEALAND
	English National Championship
	English National Leagues
	Scottish Premiership 1 & 2 (tbc)
	Scottish Premiership 3
	Scottish National Leagues 1-3
	Welsh Principality Premiership
	Swalec Welsh Nat Lges E & W
Fri. 26th to	
Sun. 28th	Magners Celtic League (9)
Sat. 27th	ENGLAND v SOUTH AFRICA
	WALES v NEW ZEALAND
	IRELAND v ARGENTINA
	SCOTLAND v SAMOA
	FRANCE v AUSTRALIA
	English National Leagues
	Scottish Premiership 1 & 2 (tbc)
	Scottish Premiership 3
	Scottish National Leagues 1-3
	Scottish Regional Bowl (1)
	Welsh Principality Premiership
	Irish Leagues 1A & B, 2, 3
Sat. 27th and	
Sun. 28th	Aviva English Premiership
	English National Championship

DECEMBER 2010

Wed. 1st	Welsh Principality Premiership
Fri. 3rd and	
Sat. 4th	Magners Celtic League (10)
Fri. 3rd to	
Sun. 5th	Aviva English Premiership
Sat. 4th	Barbarians v South Africa
	English National Championship
	English National Leagues
	Scottish Premiership 1 & 2 (tbc)
	Scottish Premiership 3
	Scottish National Leagues 1-3
	Welsh Principality Premiership
	Swalec Welsh Nat Lges E,W,N
	Irish Leagues 1A & B, 2, 3
Thu. 9th	Oxford U v Cambridge U
	Amlin Challenge Cup (3*)
Fri.10th	Aviva English Premiership
Fri. 10th to	
Sun. 12th	Heineken Cup (3)
Sat. 11th	English National Leagues
	Scottish Premiership 3
	Scottish National Leagues 1-3
	Welsh Principality Premiership
	Swalec Cup (1)
	Swalec Plate (2)
	Swalec Bowl (3)
	British & Irish Cup (1)
Sat. 11th and	
Sun. 12th	Amlin Challenge Cup (3*)
Wed. 15th	Aviva English Premiership
Thu. 16th to	
Sun. 19th	Amlin Challenge Cup (4)
Fri. 17th to	
Sun. 19th	Heineken Cup (4)
Sat. 18th	English National Leagues
	Scottish Premiership 3
	Scottish National Leagues 1-3
	Welsh Principality Premiership
	Swalec Welsh Nat Lges E,W,N
	British & Irish Cup (2)
Fri. 24th to	
Mon 27th	Magners Celtic League (11)
Sun. 26th	Aviva English Premiership
	English National Championship
	Swalec Welsh Nat Lges E & W
Mon. 27th	Aviva English Premiership
	English National Championship
	Welsh Principality Premiership
Fri. 31st to	
Sun. Jan. 2nd	Magners Celtic League (12)

JANUARY 2011

Sat. 1st	English National Championship
Sat. 1st and	
Sun. 2nd	Aviva English Premiership
Mon. 3rd	Welsh Principality Premiership
Fri. 7th to	
Sun. 9th	Magners Celtic League (13)
Sat. 8th	English National Leagues
	Scottish Premier Cup (2)
	Scottish National Shield (1)

	Scottish Regional Bowl (2)
	Welsh Principality Premiership
	Swalec Welsh Nat Lges E,W,N
Sat. 8th and	
Sun. 9th	Aviva English Premiership
	English National Championship
Thu. 13th to	
Sun. 16th	Amlin Challenge Cup (5)
Fri. 14th to	
Sun. 16th	Heineken Cup (5)
Sat. 15th	English National Leagues
	Scottish Premiership 3
	Scottish National Leagues 1-3
	Welsh Principality Premiership
	Swalec Welsh Nat Lges E,W,N
	British & Irish Cup (3)
Thu. 20th to	
Sun. 23rd	Amlin Challenge Cup (6)
Fri. 21st to	
Sun. 23rd	Heineken Cup (6)
Sat. 22nd	English National Leagues
	Scottish Premiership 3
	Scottish National Leagues 1-3
	Welsh Principality Premiership
	Swalec Welsh Nat Lges E,W,N
	British & Irish Cup (4)
Sat. 29th	LV= (Anglo-Welsh) Cup (3)
	English National Championship
	English National Leagues
	Scottish Premiership 1 & 2 (tbc)
	Scottish Premiership 3
	Scottish National Leagues 1-3
	Swalec Cup (2)
	Swalec Plate (3)
	Swalec Bowl (4)
	Irish Leagues 1A & B, 2, 3

FEBRUARY 2011

Fri. 4th	WALES v ENGLAND (19:45)
Sat. 5th	ITALY v IRELAND (14:30)
	FRANCE v SCOTLAND (17:00)
	LV= (Anglo-Welsh) Cup (4)
	Scottish Premier Cup (3)
	Scottish National Shield (2)
	Scottish Regional Bowl (3)
	Welsh Principality Premiership
	Swalec Welsh Nat Lges E,W,N
	Irish Leagues 1A & B, 2, 3
Sat. 5th and	
Sun.6th	English National Championship
Fri. 11th to	
Sun. 13th	Aviva English Premiership
	Magners Celtic League (14)
Sat. 12th	ENGLAND v ITALY (14:30)
	SCOTLAND v WALES (17:00)
	English National Championship
	English National Leagues
	Welsh Principality Premiership
	Irish Leagues 1A & B, 2, 3
Sun. 13th	IRELAND v FRANCE (15:00)
Fri. 18th to	

Sun. 20th	Aviva English Premiership
	Magners Celtic League (15)
Sat. 19th	English National Championship
	English National Leagues
	Scottish Premiership 1 & 2 (tbc)
	Scottish Premiership 3
	Scottish National Leagues 1-3
	Swalec Welsh Nat Lge N
	Swalec Cup (3)
	Swalec Plate (4)
	Swalec Bowl (5)
Fri. 25th to	
Sun. 27th	Aviva English Premiership
	Magners Celtic League (16)
Sat. 26th	ITALY v WALES (14:30)
	ENGLAND v FRANCE (17:00)
	Scottish Premier Cup play-offs
	Welsh Principality Premiership
	Irish Leagues 1A & B, 2, 3
	British & Irish Cup (5*)
Sun. 27th	SCOTLAND v IRELAND (15:00)

MARCH 2011

Fri. 4th to	
Sun. 6th	Aviva English Premiership
	Magners Celtic League (17)
Sat. 5th	English National Leagues
	Scottish Premiership 3
	Scottish National Leagues 1-3
	Welsh Principality Premiership
	Swalec Welsh Nat Lges E,W,N
	British and Irish Cup q/finals
Sat. 12th	ITALY v FRANCE (14:30)
	WALES v IRELAND (17:00)
	English National Leagues
	Scottish Premier Cup q/finals
	Scottish National Shield q/finals
	Scottish Regional Bowl q/finals
	Welsh Principality Premiership
Sat. 12th and	
Sun 13th	LV= (Anglo-Welsh) Cup s/finals
Sun. 13th	ENGLAND v SCOTLAND (15:00)
Tue. 15th	Aviva English Premiership
Sat. 19th	SCOTLAND v ITALY (14:30)
	IRELAND v ENGLAND (17:00)
	FRANCE v WALES (19:45)
	LV= (Anglo-Welsh) Cup final
	Welsh Principality Premiership
	Swalec Welsh Nat Lges E & W
Fri. 25th to	
Sun. 27th	Aviva English Premiership
	Magners Celtic League (18)
Sat. 26th	English National Leagues
	Scottish Premier Cup s/finals
	Scottish National Shield s/finals
	Scottish Regional Bowl s/finals
	Swalec Welsh Nat Lge N
	Irish Leagues 1B, 2 & 3
	U20 Championship q/finals
Sat. 26th and	
Sun. 27th	Irish League 1A

APRIL 2011

Fri. 1st to Sun. 3rd	Magners Celtic League (19)
Sat. 2nd	English National Leagues
	Scottish Premiership 1 & 2 (tbc)
	Scottish Premiership 3
	Scottish National Leagues 1-3
	Welsh Principality Premiership
	Swalec Welsh Nat Lges E,W,N
	Irish Leagues 1A & B, 3
Sat. 2nd and Sun. 3rd	Aviva English Premiership
	Irish League 2
Fri. 8th to Sun. 10th	Heineken Cup q/finals
	Amlin Challenge Cup q/finals
Sat. 9th	English National Leagues
	Swalec Welsh Nat Lges E,W,N
	Swalec Cup semi-finals
	Swalec Plate semi-finals
	Swalec Bowl semi-finals
Fri. 15th to Sun. 17th	Aviva English Premiership
	Magners Celtic League (20)
Sat. 16th	English National Leagues
	Scottish Premier Cup final
	Scottish National Shield final
	Scottish Regional Bowl final
	Welsh Principality Premiership
	Irish Leagues 2 & 3
	U20 Championship semi-finals
Fri. 22nd to Sun. 24th	Aviva English Premiership
	Magners Celtic League (21)
Sat. 23rd	English National Leagues
	British & Irish Cup semi-finals
Tue. 26th	Welsh Principality Premiership
	Play-off Championship
Sat. 30th	English Nat Championship final
	English National Leagues
	County Championship Shield (1)
Sat. 30th and Sun. 1st May	Heineken Cup semi-finals•
	Amlin Challenge Cup s/finals•

MAY 2011

Wed. 4th	Welsh Principality Premiership Play-off Championship
Fri. 6th to Sun. 8th	Magners Celtic League (22)
Sat. 7th	Aviva English Premiership
	English National League finals
	British & Irish Cup final
	Bill Beaumont Cup (1)
	County Championship Shield (2)
	U20 Championship final
	RN v The Army (Twickenham)
Wed. 11th	Welsh Principality Premiership Play-off Championship
Sat. 14th	Swalec Cup final•
	Swalec Plate final•
	Swalec Bowl final•
Sat. 14th and Sun. 15th	Aviva English P/ship s/finals
	Magners Celtic Lge s/finals•
	Bill Beaumont Cup (2)
	County Championship Shield (3)
Sat. 21st	Bill Beaumont Cup (3)
	County Championship Shield (4)
Sat. 21st and Sun. 22nd	Heineken Cup final (Cardiff)•
	Amlin Challenge Cup final•
	Emirates Airline London Sevens
Sun. 22nd	Welsh Principality Premiership Play-off Championship final
Sat. 28th	Aviva English Premiership final
	Magners Celtic League final•
	Bill Beaumont Cup final
	County Ch/ship Shield final
	County Ch/ship Plate final
	Barbarians v England Saxons

* part of (a given round)
• dates and times to be confirmed

Note: The Scottish Premier 1 & 2 season has been restructured. After their initial 11 matches (one match against each league team), they will be split into three groups of eight teams. The seven weekend 'post-split' fixtures from November 13th 2010 onwards are indicated as 'tbc' (to be confirmed).

Here's your chance to create a stir for disadvantaged children in the UK and Ireland.

Join Wooden Spoon, the childrens' charity of rugby, to help disadvantaged children and young people throughout the UK and Ireland.

Every year Wooden Spoon's members have great fun participating in a wide variety of adventures and events which raise money to provide assistance to youngsters whose circumstances are so much more difficult than our own.

Visit www.woodenspoon.com to see the many ways in which you can take part in delivering real, tangible improvements to the lives of many thousands of appreciative kids.

Membership costs just £40 per year. To apply for membership simply email members@woodenspoon.com

Donate: If membership isn't your thing, you can still make a donation by texting "SPOON" to 70700*.

www.woodenspoon.com

Wooden Spoon, 41 Frimley High St, Frimley, Surrey, GU16 7HJ
Charity Registration No. 326691 Scotland No: SC039247

Wooden Spoon
The children's charity of rugby

* A donation will cost £5 plus the cost of the text from your mobile operator. The minimum the charity will receive from your donation is £4.51